THE FRENCH REVOLUTION 1789–1989

TWO HUNDRED YEARS OF RETHINKING

THE FRENCH REVOLUTION 1789–1989

TWO HUNDRED YEARS OF RETHINKING

EDITED BY SANDY PETREY

A Special Issue of *The Eighteenth Century: Theory and Interpretation*

TEXAS TECH UNIVERSITY PRESS
1989

This book was set in 10 on 12 Baskerville and printed on acid-free paper that meets the guidelines for permanence and durability of the Committee on Production Guidelines for Book Longevity of the Council on Library Resources.

Cover design by Elaine Atkinson.

Library of Congress Cataloging-in-Publication Data

The French Revolution, 1789-1989 : two hundred years of rethinking
    edited by Sandy Petrey.
        p.   cm.
    "A special issue of The Eighteenth century :   theory and
interpretation."
    Contents: Thunder and revolution /   Marie-Hélène Huet -- Words of
change / Christie McDonald -- Aristocrate,   aristocratie / Patrice
Higgonet -- Heroism in the feminine / Chantal Thomas --
Disorder / order / James Rubin - The opening of the depths / Peter
Brooks -- French romantic histories of the revolution / Linda Orr.
    ISBN 0-89672-198-1
    1. France -- History -- Revolution, 1789-1799. 2. France -- History -
-Revolution, 1789-1799—Influence.   I. Petrey, Sandy.
DC148.F72   1989
944.04 -- dc20   89-4981
                                                                            CIP

Texas Tech University Press
Lubbock, Texas 79409-1037 U.S.A.

CONTENTS

INTRODUCTION: MEANING IN ACTION, ACTION IN MEANING

Sandy Petrey

The bicentenary of the French Revolution comes at a time of ferment in the theory and methodology of the many disciplines for which it furnishes a reference of choice. The focused concentration on semiotic forms that has characterized the human sciences since the structuralist upsurge of the 1960's is being simultaneously challenged and complemented by renewed concern for material praxis.

From one point of view, this shift constitutes the sort of return to past paradigms that makes the swing of the pendulum so recurrent a metaphor in histories of disciplinary development. Following the grand delineations of class conflict, economic organization, political structure and social movement through which the work of scholars like Mathiez and Soboul configured our ideas of the French Revolution, we came to recognize that analysis of material forces alone could never authentically explain human experience of and in history. Structuralist insistence on the abyss between the sign and the referent elicited invaluable work on sign systems as such, on the languages, festivals, narratives and plastic representations that allowed the Revolution to remake thought as well as unmake monarchy. Ideology, once an extraneous obstacle to valid apprehension of the facts of history, was recognized to be itself a fact, a historical presence with vast consequences for historical change.

Within the high structuralist model, meaning is forever incomprehensible if we assume that it proceeds directly and straightforwardly from the things it explains. To approach meaning productively demands understanding that its canny ruses are origins rather than consequences, systemic rather than derivative. The will to see through ideology to what it conceals is hopelessly misguided, for the function of ideology is to make itself coherent without regard to anything that is not itself. For a certain perspective on the human sciences, determination of the sense of past events requires accepting as axiomatic that those events contributed nothing consequential to the sense made of them.

1

Such repudiation of events is under telling attack in a number of disciplines, and this new awareness of the limitations of semiotics is an important reason why evoking the pendulum seems in order. But the articles that compose this bicentennial approach to the French Revolution illustrate why we must refrain from assuming that there is after all nothing new under the sun. Instead of moving from material reality to semiotic forms and back again, scholarship on the Revolution is invalidating the very opposition between materialism and semiotics. The recent recovery of objective reality has entailed transmuting former concepts of what constitutes an object. In the new historicism, the adjective is at least as vital as the noun.

The task now facing scholars of the French Revolution is not to choose between the production of signs and the transformation of reality but to show why every such choice misses the Revolution's achievement. In the terms of Marx's most famous thesis on Feuerbach, interpreting and changing the world are not mutually exclusive but inseparable, and the French Revolution is an inexhaustible store of evidence that this is so. Rather than returning to the idea that material history repudiates ideological distortions, much exciting work in the humanities and social sciences is spreading the conviction that ideology *is* material if we consider the material to be all that makes and unmakes the real conditions of existence. In the anaphorically emphatic terms of Louis Althusser's "Ideology and Ideological State Apparatuses," ideology is *"material actions inserted into material practices governed by material rituals."* In their constant attention to the interaction of meaning and action, politics and semantics, social change and semiotic forms, the articles collected here confirm Althusser's insistently repetitive point. We have ignored the lessons taught by the French Revolution every time we have isolated its actual nature and its symbolic representations one from the other.

Althusser is one of several thinkers whose increasingly frequent citations suggest the magnitude of current efforts to integrate formerly antagonistic schemas for apprehending the forms and facts of historical development. The thinker most invoked in the following articles, J. L. Austin, is one whose terminology and concepts provide an especially cogent instance of the analytical power established when semiotics is set firmly within social praxis. With a thoroughness suggested by the sometimes irreconcilable terms that combine to produce its name, speech-act theory repudiates every contention that words stand apart from the world, that the world stands independently of words. Austin's great insight was that words do things, and his current prominence is due largely to the resource he provides for all those who want to move from either things or words to the other without denying the interests that first drew them to the place they need to leave.

The French Revolution is replete with examples of what Austin called performative speech, language that does not say what is but transforms it. From the self-conversion of the Third Estate into the National Assembly in 1789 to the restoration and re-restoration of the Bourbon regime in 1814-1815, the years of the Revolution were a continuous illustration of the power of words to enact what their users willed. Yet each component of the illustration also demonstrates that words could perform only when their users joined in, that declaration of the end or the beginning of a world required collective determination to make the change stick.

The Revolution is also unfailingly pertinent to another of Austin's favorite themes, his argument that constative speech— language that does not overtly change reality but appears only to name it—is actually a full-fledged performance as well. For Austin, the meaning of a verbal statement is identical to the action of a verbal performance because each depends absolutely on the conventions organizing a verbal community into a social whole. Austin, Althusser, Bakhtin and his school, and an important group of other thinkers are inspiring provocative efforts to bring meaning and action together throughout the human sciences. The following essays address some of the ways the French Revolution provides those efforts with a model for analysis as well as an object to analyze.

For Patrice Higonnet, the manifold instances of the French Revolution's conversion of language into political action, as of its translation of political action into language, were encapsulated in the fortunes of a single word, *aristocrate*. The revolutionary decade was the period when the abstract philosophizing of political theorists became concrete agitation in the streets. The vocabulary of political theory shared the new worldliness of the propositions it had been used to express. The French Revolution took *aristocrate* out of the ponderous tomes that had been its only niche to make it a militant ally of masses in movement.

The semantico-political vicissitudes of *aristocrate* furnish a striking instance of the almost inverse correlation between stability of meaning and magnitude of effect that characterized the French Revolution. For all practical purposes (and those were the purposes that mattered), *aristocrate* gave no clue to the social rank of the person it designated. Applied to the lowest as well as the highest, its only constant content was that it was the antonym of *patriote*. One word named those who supported the Revolution, the other those who opposed it. As the Revolution was continually being completed and starting over, the sense of the words naming its defenders and antagonists was continually being set in stone and thrown to the winds. Semantic flux was as a consequence inseparable from pragmatic potency. If no one could define *aristocrate*, everyone could see that it was a label with awesome consequences for those to whom it was attached. The Thermidorian journalist quoted by Higonnet was exaggerating when he said that "the word *aristocrate* has all by itself killed more than three hundred thousand Frenchmen," but he was unknowingly correct in his derisive statement that revolutionary language was identical to a sorcerer's magic wand in overturning the world by uttering words. The French Revolution was explosively consistent in its determination to do things with words, and Higonnet's amusing documentation of the semantic vagaries of *aristocrate* alternates with arresting attention to the word's staggering political force.

Higonnet argues that the word *aristocrate* can even be seen as having made the Revolution "politically possible." He shares the opinion that the central aporia in Jacobin ideology was the contradiction between communal and individual needs, between private property and the public weal, and he highlights the value of the *aristocrate/patriote* binary in concealing the aporia from those it might have paralyzed. By virtue of its semantic vagueness, *aristocrate* allowed the Revolution to represent itself as starkly single-minded when it was in fact despairingly many-headed. As Higonnet summarizes the dominant thought pattern, "if aristocracy exists, patriotism must also be real." The reality of the things patriotism accomplished is not in the least diminished by the problematic nature of the words it used to inspire itself. Although the meaning of *aristocratie* could not be specified, the actions taken against it were crucial to making the modern world.

Linda Orr's study of Jules Michelet and Louis Blanc's histories of the French Revolution establishes a compelling connection between the language the Revolution used to make itself and the language subsequently used to express what was made. Orr's major concern is the intractable problematic of origins and conclusions. To capture any historical period in writing requires preliminary determination of what the period encompasses, and neither the Revolution's starting point nor its end point has ever been fixed. Yet histories of the Revolution indubitably exist—this year will see their number proliferate impressively—and as a result chroniclers have in a sense reproduced as well as recounted the revolutionary task. Orr argues that periodization establishes data as well as organizing them, and her points apply to the revolutionary's will to establish an era as well as to the historian's will to circumscribe one. For history in both senses of the term, making sense demands that the making be fully as emphatic as the sense.

As Orr listens to the "specific dismay and passion" of her two historians, she hears again and again a voice that cannot be constative without also being performative. Michelet's text "erects" a revolution, "mimes the monument it constructs." The vision of a socialist society that Blanc incorporates into his history of the triumph of the bourgeoisie must "perform" the Revolution it predicts. Both men produced a body of work that necessarily imposed "social and political hierarchies as well as hierarchies of meaning and sense." In their inability to extricate historical meaning from historical action, perception from production, the given from the fabricated, Michelet and Blanc exemplify the factors that have meant that two hundred years of rethinking remain unable to impose any form of closure on the West's obsession with the French Revolution.

Orr sets Michelet, Blanc, and Romantic historiography in general squarely within the concerns that define our own vision/experience of history along with the vision/experience of the French Revolution. French Romantic history, the "founder of our social and political sciences," also reanimates and repeats the Jacobin problematic. Or is it better to say rather that our sense of the Jacobin problematic is the *creation* of the ways historians write, that there is necessarily a feeling of repetition because the French Revolution is for us uniquely the language that has been used to represent it? Do the contradictions in revolutionary ideology reproduce themselves in historiographic structure, or does historiographic structure engender the contradictions it pretends to discover? In Orr's formulation, do we confront ontology or untology when we read about the French Revolution? If the latter, how does an untology acquire the ontological solidity being contemplated, calibrated and celebrated around the globe in 1989?

Such questions have been crucial to influential studies of the French Revolution at least since Hayden White's *Metahistory*. As Orr poses them, they foreground the interpenetration of narrative and analysis, facts and explanation, in a way that heightens attention to the prototypically Revolutionary concern with the interpenetration of semantics and politics. In the words that write history as in the words that make it, meaning and action are inextricable.

Marie-Hélène Huet's study of Franklin and Robespierre follows the interplay of meaning and action in that which both lights up the heavens and blasts the earth apart. Lightning, a natural phenomenon that calls attention to itself in the most dramatic of ways, remains a figure for human submission to uncontrollable forces even after Franklin and the lightning rod have also converted it into a figure for humanity's ability to master its destiny by dominating all that is opposed to the world it has chosen. The prevalence of storm imagery in representation of the Revolution by those who lived and narrated it prolongs the ambiguity inherent in a storm's most stirring announcement that it has arrived. Like lightning, the French Revolution is a destructive power that can nevertheless be forced to follow a path laid out in advance.

And, like the French Revolution, lightning symbolizes at once the victory and the defeat of Enlightenment thought. For Huet, the trial in which Robespierre defended the lightning rod against his recalcitrant fellow citizens is rich with language that would become pivotal to the relationships between *philosophes* and revolutionaries, between political theory and political change, between scientific reason and civic virtue. She examines the nexus of lightning and enlightenment in the Encyclopedia, Condorcet, Sade, and the Cult of the Supreme Being as well as in Franklin and Robespierre. Her theme throughout is the way the Revolution conceived itself; her conclusion with Sade's words on the lightning that kills Justine while vivifying *Justine* suggests the contradictions that gave that self-conception world-historical dynamism. In the revolutionary thunderbolt, destruction was always despairingly close to life-giving control of the destroyer.

Huet's emphasis on the contradiction in the word *laws* provides a striking instance of the Revolution's display of truth and action as mutually constitutive. As his eulogists repeated without cease, Franklin not only *revealed* the laws of electricity but also *imposed* laws on the thunderbolt. The man who saw truth was also the man who made it work, and Huet can call French descriptions of Franklin and lightning an "allegory of Revolution" because the Revolution faced the same dual task. To discover the laws of proper human interaction was but a first step; it was also necessary to give the discovery practical form, a form that could come only from a nation willing to live the law as well as perceive it. The complex links between the political and scientific orders were resolutely bidirectional, for each required that its laws be enforced as well as expressed. Turgot's epigram on Franklin, the man who seized the lightning from the heavens and the scepter from the tyrant, was so popular during the years of the Revolution because it captured the combination of understanding and upheaval that made those years revolutionary.

Christie McDonald's subject is the interplay of upheaval and articulation. The Revolution that Carlyle called the great birth-death of worlds was the great birth-death of words as well, and McDonald's analysis of the discomfiture of Guy-Jean-Baptiste Target before the National Assembly focuses on the violence that made the death of words clearly prefigure a world meeting its end. Target's error was his failure to recognize that verbal meaning is a historical construct. When history is constructing something new, old meanings cannot remain intact. A discourse that would have been the soul of propriety on August 12, 1788, was on August 12, 1789, an outburst of obscenity, and the fervor with which Target's colleagues pointed out his discursive misapprehension was to erupt repeatedly as the Revolution worked out its insights into the multiple ways saying is correlated with doing.

As Ferdinand de Saussure taught with far-reaching effect, language—*la langue*—is collective while speech—*la parole*—is individual. McDonald relates that foundational principle of general linguistics to the foundational concern with the general will that was among the Revolution's most prominent traits. Target spoke as an individual but used the language of a collectivity that could no longer impose the conventions making its language its own. In response, a different collectivity excoriated the past in the person of its spokesman, and an individual came to grief through taking for his own what in fact belonged to others. The consequence was that the National

Assembly's collective celebration of the newborn value of the individual took the disquieting form of silencing an individual, one who thought that his speech expressed his selfhood when it actually expressed the wrong collectivity. The paradox of all linguistic communication, that we must convey our most intimate being through words that are not ours, was tightly bound up with the conflict between personal desires and the general will that the French Revolution encountered in theory and practice throughout its tumultuous development.

McDonald is therefore able to use the National Assembly's dismemberment of Target's rhetoric as the base for a broad inquiry into the Revolution's reading of Rousseau and Diderot and into its efforts to educate those who were to preserve and develop its accomplishments. She sees the National Assembly as creating on August 12, 1789, "a new truth whose foundation and even verification must be found in its own acts." In the days and years that followed August 12, 1789, the creation and verification of truth were continuous, and the acts through which truth became true continue to reverberate.

Far too often, the truth the French Revolution created was gendered, the acts that verified it forbidden to women. Chantal Thomas responds to the consequences when two women, Charlotte Corday and Madame Roland, determined that they would through deeds and words live truth while debunking what had passed for it. The Revolution, and those like Michelet who chronicled its progress, often defined women as irrelevant to the forward thrust of history. The Revolution brought reason into politics, women were creatures of emotion; the Revolution gave full scope to the exercise of individual talent, women mattered only when great numbers converted them into something manly; the Revolution made the public sphere the scene of consequence, a woman's place was in the home. To laws explicitly condemning women to inferiority and subordination, the Revolution added ideological constraints that grounded woman's place in what had always been and would always be. Many of the men who entered history by explosively repudiating the notion that reality was an unchangeable given were nevertheless convinced that the status of women was due purely and simply to an eternal nature that could never be altered.

Madame Roland and Charlotte Corday refuted the age's concept of their existence as women in distinct ways. The cabinet minister's wife thought and wrote her way to the guillotine, the

Caen maiden gave her head for a single deed. Yet both mentally accepted several of the definitions of women they ridiculed in practice. Thomas highlights the eloquent writing through which Madame Roland denied that she was either eloquent or a writer, the spirited defenses of a wife's proper role made by this most un-role-governed of wives. Equally striking is the indignation that shakes Charlotte Corday when, after assassinating Marat, she realizes that she is being taken for an assassin. The poignancy of her final request that her portrait be made owes much to her "feminine" reaction to reports that she was physically ugly as well as morally reprehensible. As Thomas puts it, both women accepted in every way the masculinist ideology of their age while acting in such a way as to shred that ideology to bits. "Heroism in the feminine" was a concept that both women embodied, that neither woman announced.

Their reluctance to accept the implications of their own lives was magnified many times over among those of their contemporaries who put them to death. Because Charlotte Corday and Madame Roland broke the mold imposed on women by ideology, logic required that the defenders of ideology classify them as something other than women. Thomas's indignation at the language through which the gender change was effected is tempered by bemusement at the exaggerated intensity of the effort. Women who died heroically during the French Revolution were rabidly denied both their heroism and their womanhood. The events that demonstrated so persuasively that words could produce life-enhancing truth were also capable of converting words into life-debasing billingsgate.

In her explication of David's painting of Marat, Thomas attends to the message conveyed by the figure that is absent, that of Charlotte Corday. In his analysis of the same painting, James Rubin reacts to the figures that are present, those of Marat and of David himself. Through an explicit and sustained use of Austin's foundational definitions of constative and performative representation, Rubin defines Revolutionary art as simultaneously violating inherited conventions, asserting its right to do so in the name of historical progress, giving those conventions it preserves a new meaning for a new world, and transforming an audience in the process of performing for it. Like verbal communication, pictorial art displayed during the French Revolution an almost overt desire to impose a reality as well as denote it. David's *Marat* multiplies signals that depiction is and must be performative,

that, as Rubin argues, "the mode of representation of the
Revolution is an act of Revolution and refers to itself as such."
During the Revolution, the self-referentiality of artistic forms, so
often used in recent years to shut the work off from history, was
itself eminently historical. It powerfully figured the political
events that produced a different France by claiming the right of
art to use themselves as their own justifying ground.

In Rubin's analysis, patriotic fervor is not only the origin but
also the product of David's paintings of martyrs to the struggle
for human liberation; reality is not only that which the painter
David was charged with capturing but also that which the activist
David was charged with inculcating. Because the painter and the
activist—the painting and the action—were one, analysis of either
is condemned to sterility unless it openly incorporates the other.
David's audience was the French Revolution's support, a body
that looked at his painting and saw through artifice to the real to
the same purpose and with the same determination evident when
it saw through the old regime to a new order. Far from the naive
assumption that art provides a transparent opening onto the
world, the collective perception of Marat the man in David's
painting of him was animated by the transformative vision that
discerned a republic one and indivisible where there was also
nothing except formal arrangement of elements from a symbolic
system.

Allegory has long figured among the symbolic systems most
decisively removed from authentic representational validity. It is
therefore deliberately provocative for Rubin to complement his
analysis of the historical realism in David's *Marat* with
confirming analysis of the allegorical figures in Regnault's
Liberty or Death. The disparate genres adopted in the two
paintings impose an inverted relationship between the sensation
of reality and the painted figures through which the sensation is
conveyed; nevertheless, both paintings display the French
Revolution's adamant refusal to allow symbolic forms to remain
placidly formal. Like the *Marat, Liberty or Death* insistently
interpellated the subjects that viewed it. The ideas written into its
paint were as horrific to the Revolution's opponents as they were
inspiriting to its supporters. The parallels Rubin establishes
between reactions of contemporary viewers before the two
paintings are fully as striking as the formal qualities that make
the works incommensurable. While the conventions applied were
indeed disparate, the two works constitute a single demonstration

of Austin's insights into the mutually invigorating relationship of conventions observed and reality lived.

Innovative literary conventions were also a feature of the French Revolution, despite the cliché that the revolutionary decade is a nearly blank space in the history of French literature. Peter Brooks examines an innovation that was to display extraordinary durability, melodrama, and inquires into the ways the melodramatic form articulates a *psychological* danger that the Revolution's obsession with *political* change left unremarked. Like McDonald and Higonnet, Brooks sees collective and individual impulses as far from coincident; he addresses the problems left in the dark when liberation is conceived as a wholly positive entry into the purest light.

The proto-melodramas that compulsively and repetitively represented the French Revolution as freeing humanity from the dungeon all built a common contradiction into their theatrical structure: if they took their characters up from the darkest depths of claustration into the open air of liberty, they took their audiences in the opposite direction. To enter the theater was to go down into the pit, and the audiences produced by the French Revolution showed an insatiable desire to do just that. In Brooks's image, those responsible for maintaining the ideals of the Age of Reason were irresistibly attracted to the monsters engendered by the sleep of reason.

Brooks concludes his Freudian analysis of the intersection of melodrama and revolution with the works of the marquis de Sade, an author who also appears importantly in the different approaches to the French Revolution made here by Chantal Thomas and Marie-Hélène Huet. Brooks's treatment parts from the fact that Sade "brings his most sustained analytic attention to the Revolution" in one of his most sustained synthetic elaborations of debauchery, *Philosophy in the Bedroom*. Sade's work consequently embodies the configuration Brooks presents as uniting revolutionary liberation, unending imprisonment, and the outburst of repressed desire. It is arguable that Sade and melodrama are the French Revolution's most influential contributions to world literature. Brooks's essay suggests the psychic mechanisms responsible for the almost transhistorical pertinence of the literary expressions arising from this most historicized of events.

All the articles comprising this special issue of *The Eighteenth Century: Theory and Interpretation* are comparably concerned

with the historical and the permanent. Each addresses a specific
aspect of the French Revolution, the broad sequence of which
determines the order of the articles' appearance here. Each also
speculates on the general lessons that can be drawn from their
specific topic, lessons that converge into a view of meaning in
action, of signs in history, that is very much of our own age.
Two centuries after it began, the French Revolution remains the
timeliest of topics.

THUNDER AND REVOLUTION:
FRANKLIN, ROBESPIERRE, SADE

Marie-Hélène Huet

Lightning long stood as the privileged metaphor for divine vengeance; the scientist, a modern Prometheus, thus presented himself as braving great danger to wrest from heaven the power of a knowledge that, like lightning, brings light and death at once. The first version of the article *Thunder* in the *Encyclopedia*, published in 1756, provides the following information on how to protect oneself from lightning:

> The thunderbolt can be broken up or turned away by the sound of several large bells or by shooting a cannon; this stimulates in the air a great agitation that disperses the thunderbolt into its separate parts; but it is essential to take care not to toll the bells when the cloud is directly overhead, for then the cloud may split and drop its thunderbolt. In 1718, lightning struck twenty-four churches in lower Brittany, in the coastal region extending from Landerneau to Saint-Paul de Léon; it struck precisely those churches where the bells were tolling to drive it away; neighboring churches where the bells were not tolling were spared.[1]

This text clearly shows the two principles that simultaneously mediate and limit the power given by human knowledge: the church on the one hand, the essentially whimsical character of untamed nature on the other. The exercise of knowledge—that the sound of bells drives lightning away—is here immediately punished, with almost divine scope, in the very sites humans have constructed to worship their God. The silent steeples spared by the storm can conversely serve as metaphor for a religious but ignorant people, unconcerned with understanding Heaven, forever resigned and here rewarded for their blind submission.

This article from the *Encyclopedia* obviously does not take account of the theories on lightning Benjamin Franklin published in London in 1751 under the title *Experiments and Observations on Electricity.*[2] Preliminary application of Franklin's theories would come a year later and take a variety of forms, such as the kite or the "fulminating bars" of Thomas François Dalibard in France. But the 1777 *Supplement* to the *Encyclopedia* does full justice to Franklin's invention and ingenuity. The second *Thunder* article has this to say:

> It is a truth now recognized by all physicists that the matter which flames up
> in clouds, which produces lightning and thunderbolts, is nothing other than
> electric fire; the famous Franklin assembled the proofs of this in his fifth
> letter on electricity . . . M. Franklin proposed as early as 1750 to use these
> means [electric kites, fulminating bars and other sorts of apparatus] to protect
> buildings and ships from lightning; observations have proven so successful
> that it is now of interest to explain, in a way everyone can understand, how
> to build these conductors or *lightning rods*.[3]

There follows an imposing list of individuals and institutions
that have successfully installed lightning rods. The article's
author was none other than Guyton de Morveau, a distinguished
chemist who was later to play an active role in the Revolution.[4]
However, despite the eloquent demystification of lightning given
in the *Supplement*, popular superstition was still alive and well
in 1780, when there took place in Arras a celebrated trial in
which Maximilien de Robespierre, then a very young lawyer,
came to defend Franklin's principles.[5] The trial, much commented on, is of interest not only because it unites the names of
Marat, Condorcet, Franklin and Robespierre some years before
the Revolution but also because it involves a debate on
Enlightenment and religion, science and human progress, that
was to continue until Robespierre's death.

Here are the circumstances of the trial. In 1780, a lawyer from
Saint-Omer, Monsieur de Vissery de Bois-Valé, installed a
lightning rod on his roof. His frightened neighbors sought
redress, convinced that the lightning rod, like the tolling bells of
Saint-Paul de Léon, was more likely to strike them dead than to
protect them from the storm. On June 14, 1780, the magistrates
of Saint-Omer ordered the lightning rod removed within twenty-
four hours. On June 16, Monsieur de Vissery submitted to the
court a petition "accompanied by a special report, the object of
which was to furnish the judges with a complete demonstration
of the electrical machine placed above his house."[6] Arguments
were heard on June 21, and Monsieur de Vissery's petition was
denied. Two days later, he appealed to the Artois council, after
agreeing in the interval to take down the apparatus so distressing
to the population. In fact, he did nothing more than remove the
sword blade that was the most visible part and substitute a
shorter blade. And, so that no one should see even this concession
as a symbolic abasement of the ruling class, Vissery confided to
his lawyer that "This is how to deal with the ignorant masses."[7]

Monsieur de Vissery entrusted the affair to Antoine-Joseph
Buissart,[8] then a member of the Arras and Dijon Academies who

FIGURE. 1. Expérience de Benjamin Franklin sur le paratonnerre (Boyer 30807). Cliché Roger-Viollet. Reproduced by permission.

regularly collaborated on the *Journal de Physique*. Buissart took the affair to heart, and interminable consultations took place throughout France. The man slowest to answer Buissart's reiterated requests was Jean-Antoine-Nicolas Caritat, marquis de Condorcet, who nevertheless finally let it be known that, speaking as the Perpetual Secretary of the Academy of Sciences, he considered the best defense to be a detailed and documented report containing all the scientific arguments in favor of the lightning rod. Buissart published his report in 1782, and the appeal finally reached the Council of Artois in May of 1783.[9] That is when Buissart gave Robespierre the task of presenting to the Court the combined interests of science and Monsieur de Vissery.

Robespierre made two speeches that took their scientific content, their examples, and a part of their logic from the work to which Buissart had devoted two years. Yet the final formulation is that of the young lawyer, who published his two speeches under the title *Arguments for the Sieur de Vissery de Bois-Valé, appealing a judgement of the magistrates of Saint-Omer, who had ordered that a lightning rod erected on his house be destroyed.*[10] Emboldened by his success (on May 31, the Council of Artois found in favor of Robespierre's position), the lawyer sent a copy of his arguments to Franklin, along with a letter that, although often quoted, deserves another hearing. It is dated October 1, 1783, four months after its author's striking success, and less than two months before a new opposition was again to threaten Monsieur de Vissery's lightning rod. Robespierre wrote:

Sir,
A writ of condemnation by the magistrates of Saint-Omer against electrical conductors furnished me the opportunity to appear before the Council of Artois and plead the cause of a sublime discovery for which the human race owes you its thanks. The desire to help root out the prejudices that opposed its extension in our province led me to publish the speeches I made during this affair. I dare hope, Sir, that you will deign to have the goodness to accept a copy of this work, the object of which was to induce my fellow citizens to accept one of your gifts: happy to have been useful to my country by persuading its first magistrates to welcome this important discovery; happier still if I can add to this advantage that of being honored by the good graces of a man whose least merit is to be the most illustrious scientist of the universe. I have the honor of being with respect, Sir, your most humble and obedient servant.[11]

In this rather conventional letter, to which Franklin undoubtedly never replied, one expression should be carefully noted: Electricity is a "sublime discovery." For Robespierre the word *sublime*, in a way that he will make more explicit in his future speeches to the Convention, is synonymous with *sacred*. Not *sacred* in the "religious" sense—Robespierre, like Rousseau, distrusted any ecclesiastical institutions that could mediate the primordial relationship between man and God—but *sublime* insofar as "divine."[12] Once again, the Promethean relationship between science and the sacred comes to the fore.

In the France of the 1780s, Franklin's glory was at its apogee. He was the man of the lightning rod and of the American revolution, a double achievement Turgot admirably captured in a Latin epigram: "Eripuit coelo fulmen, sceptrumque tyrannis."[13] This epigram was tremendously popular. It appeared in 1778 under the bust of Franklin sculpted by Jean-Baptiste Houdon, and it was the beginning of countless poetic essays to the glory of the American scientist and politician. In an especially interesting exchange of letters between d'Alembert and Jean-Baptiste Suard, the encyclopedist undertook to translate Turgot's epigram and hesitated between two versions. D'Alembert suggested this quatrain: "Tu vois le sage courageux/ Dont l'heureux et mâle génie/ Arracha le tonnerre aux dieux/ Et le sceptre à la tyrannie." D'Alembert added that it would be possible to say either that Franklin wrested lightning from the skies or from the gods, *aux cieux* or *aux dieux*.[14] This hesitation, as to whether the conquest of lightning is a victory over nature or whether it is a triumph over a more sacred principle, recalls the two *Thunder* articles in the *Encyclopedia*. All knowledge is a seizure of power, a deed of the same stamp as political revolution. Turgot's epigram, d'Alembert's double translation, and the Saint-Omer trial therefore form an ideological nexus structured by the Enlightenment's connection to science as well as the Enlightenment's contribution to the Revolution. In these heated and often contradictory debates, a recurrent series of metaphors put lightning and enlightenment into play.

A Distant Thunder

In a work entitled *Clartés et ombres au siècle des Lumières*,[15] Roland Mortier traces the history of the philosophical meaning of the word *lumières* from Genesis to Kant's celebrated *Was ist Aufklärung?* He notes in particular how, in the seventeenth century, the use of *lumières* was secularized. If Furetière could still write that "The Enlightenment of Faith and the Gospels have dissipated the shadows and the blindness of the human race," the word was already inscribed in a semantic system that associated it with reason and opposed it to ignorance. Examples are abundant in Malebranche, and the metaphor of Enlightenment as reasoned knowledge would become general in the eighteenth century. The *Encyclopedia* provided the metaphor's richest expression; here, far from association with revealed knowledge of a religious nature, Enlightenment was directly opposed to all knowledge transmitted or authorized, in the strict sense of the term, by the Church. Diderot contrasted an "enlightened century" to "times of darkness and ignorance." Voltaire suggested that "a Gothic government snuffed out all enlightenment for almost 1200 years." D'Alembert congratulated himself that "enlightenment has prevailed in France."[16]

Turgot, who was to become intimate with Franklin in Paris, evolved from thinking that he could preach the reconciliation of Church, Royalty, and Enlightenment—"Great is the advantage to kings and governments when the people are enlightened"[17]—to thinking that Enlightenment provided access to a natural religion. Enlightenment acquired a resolutely profane meaning. Outside this movement, Rousseau alone was to strive to reopen the question of Enlightenment as opposed not to ignorance and religious traditions but to the notions of virtue and truth. In Rousseau's view, Enlightenment was a dangerous snare, and the debate he began would continue throughout the Revolution, itself often divided between the Republic of Arts and Sciences and the Republic of Virtue.

His legal arguments on the lightning rod gave Robespierre the opportunity to develop his own version of the already classical metaphor of Enlightenment. Ridiculing his opponents, he proclaimed, "How dangerous to want to *enlighten* one's fellow citizens! Ignorance, prejudices and passions have formed an awesome front against men of genius, in order to punish them for the good they do their fellows." Elsewhere Robespierre celebrated "the progress of enlightenment," "enlightened nations," "the torch of arts," and "the torch of true principles."[18]

The description of lightning and thunderbolts would moreover serve to illustrate the complex relationship between Enlightenment and Nature. In fact, this relationship is a contradiction. Lightning is actually the prime example of a power *without reason* that strikes *blindly*. Lightning is barbarity is nature. While describing Franklin's discovery, Robespierre explained: "Lightning accepted its laws and thereby immediately lost this *blind* and irresistible impulse to strike, smash, overturn, crush all that stands in its way; it has learned to recognize the objects it is to spare."[19] By its brightness, lightning blinds; itself a blind force, it destroys indiscriminately. It is for the true Enlightenment

to tame this energy and submit nature to its laws. Robespierre
sets out to demonstrate simultaneously—here he is not at all
Rousseau's disciple[20]—the savage, raw and noxious character of
nature, and in contrast the purely beneficent character of science
and reason. To illustrate the lightning rod's virtues, Robespierre
compares it to inoculation, itself far from unanimously accepted
by scientists. "We must calculate," he said, "the victims art has
saved and those nature has sacrificed; but, because this
calculation generally proved that men gain more from confiding
themselves to art than from giving themselves to nature,
inoculation has triumphed over all obstacles."[21]

In the opposition he was sketching between Enlightenment and
nature, Robespierre demystified the idea of an inspired nature,
the manifestation of a benevolent and hidden God whose secrets
were to remain forever closed to humanity. Did this mean that
science took the place of a deposed God? That Enlightenment
would guide humanity as the sacred word had once done? Not at
all, and this is perhaps the most interesting point in Robespierre's arguments: humans must no more let themselves be dazzled
by science than by the lightning that threatens to strike them
dead. This is in fact the lawyer's most extensively developed
theme. Comparing the arrival of Enlightenment to the conquest
of the Americas, Robespierre exclaimed:

> The enlightened European had become a God for the savage inhabitants of
> America; I call those peoples as witness, for they gave no other name to their
> conquerors. Were they so very wrong? Was not lightning in the hands of these
> terrible warriors? Was not their very arrival in those unknown regions a
> prodigious deed accomplished to justify such an idea? And, whether they
> descended from Heaven, as in the opinion of the inhabitants of that savage
> country, or opened a road across the immensity of the seas, braving the fury
> of the waves, commanding the tempest, subjugating a fearsome element, is
> not either *miracle* far beyond the strength of human beings?[22]

But only the ignorant see in nature a divine force, only they see
in the conquest of nature—as of the Americas—the manifestation
of divine or godlike knowledge. In his second speech, Robespierre
dwelt at length on the idea that science rightly understood is no
more extraordinary, no more frightening, no more divine than
lightning explained by Franklin:

> The effects of lightning rods, so you have heard, are so miraculous that men
> are right to be wary of them. Man commanding the thunderbolt! Tracing the
> route it must follow! Is this phenomenon plausible? Is it not natural to see it
> at first as a shimmering illusion brought to life by the pride of the human
> mind? The effects of lightning rods are too prodigious to earn our
> confidence! ... Is man so unfamiliar with miracles that another prodigy

leaves him stupefied? Have the Sciences produced for his benefit few miracles
that he must consider this new boon beyond their power? . . . But what am I
saying? *There is no miracle here.* That man has dared wrest the lightning
from heaven; that he controls all its movements however he chooses; that he
says to it: be careful not to touch these buildings; come, follow the route I
have set for you, and hasten to bury yourself in the abyss I have made for
you; there is a prodigy: *but it is also nothing more than a product of the
imagination.* The Poet or the Orator, animated by a fitting enthusiasm, has
the right to deploy such brilliant figures. But when we examine this
phenomenon as a physicist, *the miracle vanishes.* In the place of lightning,
which escapes from eternal hands to pass into those of men, I see nothing
except a quantity of electrical matter . . . which betakes itself . . . toward a
metal ban. . . . Is that a prodigy? No, it is a law of nature, it is an ordinary
phenomenon.[23]

There is neither an avenging God nor a Promethean scientist;
those, Robespierre tells us, are poetic figures. Perhaps the basic
difference between poetry and science is to be found, rhetorically,
in the poet's "right" to transform a simple mechanical process
into a prodigy and to use fear of a barbarous nature to produce
the language of lightning and blindness.

But now, in the Age of Enlightenment, there is no miracle in
dominating Nature, for Heaven is emptied of an avenging God.
"Neither let us be afraid that Heaven will see this step as an
audacious effort to defy its anger, to take from it the power to
punish our crimes. Do we believe that the Omnipotent needs this
meteor that terrifies us, that without it His weaponless arm could
no longer strike us?"[24] If there is an opposition between the blind
force of nature and the rational laws of science, there is no
incompatibility between a reasonable God and Enlightenment.
On the contrary, the first speech for the defense begins with this
declaration: "The Arts and Sciences are the richest gift that
Heaven has made to men"—another principle quite foreign to
Rousseau, and which Robespierre nonetheless never abandoned.
Just as Providence has given us simples to cure us, "Today she
presents us with electrical conductors to protect us from the
ravages of lightning."[25] This is precisely why Franklin's discovery
is *sublime.* The Sciences perform no miracles, they are the fruit
of a reason that itself emanates from God.

THE REVOLUTIONARY STORM

Mary Wollstonecraft described the Revolution of 1789 as similar
in its convulsions to "hurricanes, whirling over the face of
nature."[26] The revolutionary tempest broke over Paris some years
after the lightning rod trial. Richard Price, even more explicit

than Mary Wollstonecraft, exclaimed, "Behold, the light you
have struck out, after setting America free, reflected in France,
and there kindled into a blaze that lays despotism in ashes, and
warms and illuminates all Europe."[27] The Revolution of 1789
becomes like the thunderbolt lightning that Franklin, far from
mastering, unleashed to spread from America to Europe. The
torch of Reason set the powder afire, and if Nature was for an
instant dominated by Reason, human nature is to be unleashed
in such a way that no reason will ever be able to arrest it. Two
questions are therefore put to Robespierre and his contemporaries: was Enlightenment responsible for the revolutionary storm?
Can there be a political revolution without a philosophical
revolution? From these two questions proceed two thoughts on
what every revolution must be. And here again Franklin was to
act as a catalyst in a debate with consequences that would weigh
heavily on the fate of the Revolution.

Franklin's death was dramatically announced to the National
Assembly on June 11, 1790.[28] In a brief and eloquent speech,
Mirabeau asked the Assembly to wear mourning for three days in
honor of the American patriot. Several eulogies were printed in
the following months. The text of one homage ended with this
paragraph: "Franklin's last wish was that no inscription decorate
his tomb; but his illustrious name, which nothing could take
from him, will always be his tomb's most beautiful decoration.
Let a pyramid be raised there, with one of its sides showing the
initials of the United States intertwined with those of the French
Republic, and topped by the attributes of liberty and equality; on
the other face, let there be an electrical conductor stretching into
the clouds."[29] Condorcet's eulogy, more ideological, established
the indispensable link between Enlightenment and Revolution:
"When, through the progress of enlightenment, a real science
replaced systems, and a philosophy founded on nature and
observation succeeded scholastic prejudices, enlightened men of
all nations began to form a single body, guided by the same
principles and marching toward a common goal. Then reason
and liberty had everywhere peaceful apostles, independent in
their opinions but united in the cult they maintained for these
benevolent divinities."[30] What is more, added Condorcet, there
can be no successful revolution without enlightenment. Any
revolution showing contempt for the sciences would be like a
destructive storm, without benefit for humanity. This passionate
call for an enlightened regime also shows the magnitude of the

gap opened as early as 1790 between the Revolution and the
philosophes:

> Is there anyone who has yet to see that the people need not choose between
> cultivating the sciences and struggling under the yoke of prejudices? For, *in
> the natural order political enlightenment walks in the path of the sciences,
> depends on their progress, or else, as in antiquity, it produces only an
> uncertain, ephemeral flame, flickering in the storm*. Let us beware of those
> envious detractors who dare accuse the sciences of thriving under despotism:
> without doubt, they sense confusedly that nations deprived of enlightenment
> are easier to deceive and lead astray; that the more a people is enlightened,
> the more its support is difficult to retain unworthily. They fear the patriotism
> of reason and virtue, that which hypocrisy can neither counterfeit nor
> mislead; and, concealing the desire to dominate under the mask of
> enthusiasm for liberty, they seem to have guessed that, even under the freest
> constitution, an ignorant people is always composed of slaves.[31]

Franklin's reputation was on the increase throughout the
Revolution: engravings and prints represent him as a trustworthy
guide. His bust was honored along with those of Voltaire and
Rousseau during the great festivals.[32] Although Franklin had
been on excellent terms with the court during his stay in Paris,
his role in the American Revolution endowed him with
unparalleled prestige. If ever a scientist could make a link in the
popular imagination between revolutionary integrity and the
progress of Enlightenment, Franklin was that man. But his
friends the *philosophes* had become suspect. In April 1792, at the
Jacobin Club, Robespierre strongly attacked Condorcet. Brissot
spoke for the defense in these terms: "Do you not see that it is
only because the burning geniuses of these men [Condorcet,
Voltaire, d'Alembert] set fire to soul after soul ... that today's
tribune can ring with your speeches on liberty? You lacerate
Condorcet when his life is but one long sacrifice for the
people."[33]

But Robespierre was intractable. Having himself once pleaded
the cause of science, he remembered quite well that the first
beneficiaries of great discoveries are usually those with great
fortunes: "All Princes seem to have taken it as their duty to show
the value [of lightning rods] by example, by using them to
protect their palaces."[34] All the examples Buissart furnished
Robespierre were in fact cathedrals, powder magazines, and the
dwellings of monarchs. If Franklin stood above criticism, thanks
to his glorious role in the American Revolution, such was not the
case for the Encyclopedists. They had too often enjoyed the
support of Catherine the Great and Frederick II not to
compromise their political reputation. Condorcet himself, in his

eulogy of Franklin, had mentioned the connection between kings and philosophers: "At times enlightenment came down from the throne to the people; most often it went up from the people to the throne."[35] But for Robespierre, Enlightenment, far from leading the people to democracy, was suspect for having too long consorted with tyrants: "If our intellectual leaders are academicians, friends of d'Alembert, I have nothing to say except that the new regime's reputation cannot rest on older reputations; if d'Alembert and his friends ridiculed priests, they were sometimes cozy with kings and great personages."[36] Despite their disagreement, we might say that Robespierre and Condorcet, although differently, both contest the idea that the Enlightenment influenced the Revolution. For Condorcet, who, like Diderot, conceived history within the natural order, political enlightenment follows philosophical enlightenment not in a relation of *cause* to effect but in an inescapable sequence inscribed in nature and in the nature of history. For Robespierre, closer here to Rousseau, philosophical enlightenment, however desirable it may be, had made common cause with despotism and could in no way be considered the forerunner of the Revolution.

But the real question setting Robespierre and Condorcet at odds is this: can there be a political revolution without a philosophical revolution? Condorcet would with his usual passion repeat that an enlightened revolution alone was capable of succeeding and effecting the people's happiness. His *Esquisse d'un tableau historique des progrès de l'esprit humain* says so repeatedly. Not only do the arts and sciences enrich one another, but the political progress marching in their path is irreversible: "We will point out that the principles of philosophy, the maxims of freedom, the knowledge of man's true rights and real interests, are spread through too great a number of nations, and direct in each the opinions of too great a number of enlightened men, for there to be any prospect that they will ever fall back into oblivion."[37]

Robespierre would never question the idea of the progress of the human mind. One of his last speeches (18 floréal, an II; May 7, 1794) again took up his theme in the Saint-Omer trial: "A world has appeared beyond the boundaries of the world; the inhabitants of the earth have added the seas to their vast domain; man has conquered lightning and exorcised it from heaven." After this direct homage to Franklin, Robespierre continued, "Compare the imperfect language of hieroglyphs to the miracle

of printing; set the voyage of the argonauts next to that of La
Peyrouse; calculate the distance between the astronomical
observations of the magi of Asia and Newton's discoveries, or
between the sketch from the hand of Dibutade and the paintings
of David." Then he concluded, "Everything has changed in the
physical order; everything *must* change in the moral and political
order. Half the revolution of the world is already done; the other
half *must* be accomplished."[38]

It could not be more clearly and succinctly stated: one
revolution allows the other, *but it does not necessarily produce it.*
That is the difference between Condorcet and Robespierre.
Political revolution is not at all made by philosophers; for
Robespierre the only historical necessity is moral. As an act of
will, as the mastery of passion parallel with the mastery of
nature, Robespierre's revolution owes the *philosophes* everything,
but it does not *result* from their work. On the contrary, the
unequal development of enlightenment and political progress
opened a dangerous gap, a dangerous imbalance between
scientific ideas and moral ideas: "The peoples of Europe have
made astonishing progress in what are named the arts and
sciences, and they seem to ignore the first principles of public
morality. They know everything, except their rights and their
duties. What causes this mixture of genius and stupidity? The
answer is that, in order to make ourselves adept in the arts, we
need only follow our passions, while we must conquer them in
order to defend our rights and respect the rights of others. There
is also another reason: the kings who make the destiny of the
earth fear neither great geometers, nor great painters, nor great
poets, and they dread stern philosophers who defend humanity."[39] Robespierre bitterly attacked the Encyclopedists for having
had the power to frighten kings but choosing instead to negotiate
with them: "They fought against the Revolution the instant they
came to fear that it would raise up the people. . . . In general,
men of letters dishonored themselves in this Revolution, and, to
the eternal shame of the intellect, the reason of the people had to
pay for this."[40]

In this same speech, Robespierre presented the fundamental
ideas of the Cult of the Supreme Being. He attacked two enemies
simultaneously: the faithful of the old religion who had said to
the kings, "You are the images of God on earth,"[41] and the
Encyclopedists who had made Reason their only God. Atheism
and Catholicism were equally dangerous, and Robespierre took

up once more, and with the same firmness, the basic argument he
had used for the lightning rod trial: science does not perform
miracles. Man's conquests of nature are a victory of reason that in
no way calls the idea of a Supreme Being into question: "How
different is the God of nature from the God of priests! He knows
nothing so close to atheism as the religions they have made. By
disfiguring the Supreme Being, they annihilated Him to the best
of their abilities; they sometimes made Him a globe of fire,
sometimes an ox, sometimes a tree, sometimes a man, sometimes
a king."[42]

The relationship between science and revolution is made still
more complicated by the conflicting uses of the word *law*, among
the *philosophes* on the one hand, and Robespierre on the other.
All scientific discoveries are in fact described in terms of imposed
rules. The many epigrams greeting invention of the lightning rod
almost all contain this use of the word *law*. The attorney Target:
"Le voilà ce mortel, dont l'heureuse industrie/ Au tonnerre
imposa des *lois*" ("There is the mortal whose industry successfully imposed *laws* on the thunderbolt"). Du Pont de Nemours:
"C'est Franklin, ce mortel dont l'heureuse industrie/
Sut enchaîner la foudre et lui donner des *loix*" ("Here is Franklin, the mortal whose industry succeeded in chaining up
lightning and giving it *laws*"). Hilliard d'Auberteuil: "Si Jupiter
veut nous reduire en poudre,/ Sage Franklin, tu lui précis tes
loix" ("If Jupiter wants to blast us to bits, wise Franklin, you
remind him of your *laws*").[43]

In 1791, Vicq d'Azir's *Eloge de Franklin* described the
invention of the lightning rod in these terms:

> Torrents of light inundate space and, variously transformed, light produces
> fire, that soul of nature which vivifies, destroys, recomposes and moves
> all . . . Franklin perceives that these effects are due to electric matter; he
> analyzes it, understands it, dares attack it in the cloud that bears it. Along the
> conductor he presents to it, lightning will descend *submissive to the law
> governing it, and tame to the hand guiding it*; the anger of heaven will seem
> to be pacified; the atmosphere will again become calm and pure; from their
> refuge men and fearful flocks will again emerge, and the earth will bless the
> mortal who had this daring thought and offered it such a boon.[44]

This reads, indeed, as an allegory of Revolution. For the
Encyclopedists as for Condorcet, the political order is an
extension of the scientific order. Just as man has learned to
subdue the tempest, he will learn to subdue tyrants. Scientific law
anticipates political law and serves as its model; it emerges from
reason, is enlightened by knowledge, and strives for the good of

humanity. For Robespierre, however, the laws scientists impose on nature give them a power that is a usurpation, for it does not come from the people. Any invention not immediately put in the service of the people, any law, any power serving the privileged classes is a form of political tyranny. The people are sovereign, and the principle of the people's sovereignty transcends the principle of the progress of enlightenment. Thus the speech of April 24, 1793, on the new Declaration of Rights contains these words: "The law is the free and solemn expression of the people's will."[45] Enlightenment merely liberated the philosophical realm: "You are fortunate to live in an age and in a nation where enlightenment has so progressed that your only task is to recall men to nature and to truth."[46]

Condorcet died in mysterious circumstances—assassination, death from exhaustion, or suicide—in the spring of 1794.[47] Ropespierre was executed in July of the same year. In much the same way as Robespierre had engaged in an implicit dialogue with Franklin during his entire career, first as a lawyer, then as a revolutionary leader, in 1794 Sade began a dialogue with Robespierre which marks an ironic conclusion to the debate, begun fifteen years earlier, on the question of Revolution and Enlightenment. Sade had been secretary—president of the Section des Piques (Robespierre's section) but had been arrested at the end of 1793. From jail, he wrote a text that is largely a response to Robespierre's Cult of the Supreme Being. In *Yet another effort, Frenchmen, if you would become republicans*, Sade promptly chose Enlightenment over both law and religion: "Without laws and religions human knowledge would today be at an unimaginable height of glory and greatness; to an unmeasurable degree, these unworthy brakes have held back progress. . . . It is only in the moment of the laws' silence that great actions burst forth."[48] But the fate of Enlightenment was for Sade not at all to promote political progress or shape political law on the model of scientific law. Enlightenment was an end in itself. Sade's thought is perhaps even more radical if we see in Justine's repeated death a strangely anachronistic proclamation that knowledge is not a law and does not itself impose any law. It is only pleasure.

In 1787, the virtuous heroine who refused both pleasure and knowledge died, brutally stuck down by a thunderbolt:

> Madame de Lorsange, terribly afraid of lightning, begs her sister to close everything as fast as she can; M. de Corville was returning at that moment. Justine, rushing to calm her sister, flies to a window, she tries briefly to struggle against the wind pushing it back, just then a burst of lightning

strikes her down in the middle of the salon and leaves her lifeless on the floor. . . . The thunderbolt had gone in through the right breast, burned the chest, and gone back out through the mouth, so disfiguring the face that she was horrible to see.[49]

In the second version of *Justine*, M. de Corville, whom Sade identifies as the character who "truly knows the heart of man and the spirit of the law," is just as powerless to save the victim "struck in such wise hope itself can no longer subsist for her; the lightning entered her right breast, found the heart, and after having consumed her chest and face, burst out through her belly. The miserable thing was hideous to look upon.[50] Madame de Lorsange draws a double conclusion that also serves as the novel's epigraph. After exclaiming that the "caprices of Heaven's hand are enigmas it is not for us to sound," she adds that "the prosperity of Crime . . . is like unto the lightning, whose traitorous brilliancies but for an instant embellish the atmosphere, in order to hurl into death's very deeps the luckless one they have dazzled."[51] The enigma of Heaven: this is the object of knowledge; or rather knowledge is the recognition that heaven is beyond all knowledge, and thus beyond all law. In 1794, Sade wrote, "Let a simple philosopher instruct these new pupils in the *incomprehensible sublimities* of nature."[52] The lightning metaphor accompanies a thought that also expresses itself in terms of veils and blindness. "If it is true," he says, "that passions *blind*, that their effect is to raise before our eyes a *cloud* that disguises from us the dangers with which passions are surrounded, how can we suppose that distant dangers, like the punishments announced by your God, could ever manage to dissipate this *cloud* impervious even to the sword of the laws always hanging over passions?"[53] A disturbing paradox: lightning becomes like the passion it spares, it is *blind*, and for that reason it acts like the passion of an incomprehensible Providence, it becomes the cruel parody of a law that strikes down virtue—like the steeples of Saint-Paul de Léon—with terrifying magnitude. What lightning illuminates for an instant is immediately so disfigured that it is no longer recognizable. Thus lightning signals another frontier of knowledge, an absolute limit, far beyond the reason that lights our way and the passion that blinds us.

But above all, and this is what interest us here, Sade suggests another sort of opposition. Enlightenment is not opposed to ignorance or religion as the lightning rod to superstition. Enlightenment is opposed to shadows and fear: "Man is afraid in the dark, physically and morally as well," he states simply.[54] We might say that with this sentence, Sade distances himself from the thought of the XVIIIth century, whose encyclopedic obsession he represented elsewhere with a kind of fanaticism, and that he was already announcing a Romantic interpretation of the question of Enlightenment. Man is not afraid *of* the dark but *in* the dark. The primordial fear of the night surrounding him is still present and remains determinant even under the ephemeral brightness of reason.

We might perhaps also say that this evocation was already implicitly inscribed in the first *Thunder* article of the *Encyclopedia*. That the monuments consecrated to God, raised toward the heavens in the supplication of the bells, are the very ones pitilessly struck by lightning is not entirely explained by theories about the mass of the clouds. The fallen steeples, like Justine, illustrate a Sadean logic of the blindness of Providence and the limits of Promethean defiance. The refusal Sade opposes to the laws may come less from their being, in Blanchot's expression, "abased by precepts,"[55] or from their positing a criminal humanity ("As for me," said Sade, "I will not submit to any law that assumes I am ungrateful and corrupted"[56]) than from the fact that they imitate a natural model that does not exist. Justine's repeated deaths may signal among other things the collapse of a system. "In six months," Sade wrote in the spring of 1794, "it will all be over."[57] These words may allude to the predictable failure of the Cult of the Supreme Being, and, quite possibly, to the end of the Revolutionary fervor that disappeared with Robespierre on 9 Thermidor. Yet this announcement may also signal that the passionate debate among *philosophes* and politicians on the relationship between scientific progress and Revolution would, too, be a thing of the past. Franklin had incarnated the ideal figure of the enlightened man, dedicated to both scientific knowledge and revolutionary thought; but this ideal would soon lose priority to darker and more pressing concerns. In the Spring of 1794, Sade's vigorous opposition to Robespierre's religious program, his eloquent refusal of the republican definition of law, and his repeated evocations of nature as the blind force that strikes down virtue and spares vice, offer a violent rebuttal to the scientific discourse which had successfully imposed its laws on thunder, and to the revolutionary discourse which had placed such emphasis on virtue. It suggests, among other things, the end of Enlightenment.

NOTES

1. A Neufchastel, 16:412. The author quotes Newton, Wallis and Chambers in this article and associates the conflagration of lightning with that of gunpowder.

2. On Franklin's experiments with electricity, cf. Alfred Owen Aldridge, *Benjamin Franklin, Philosopher and Man* (Philadelphia, 1965), Chapter 9, "The Electrical Years," 91-101. See also Esmond Wright, *Franklin of Philadelphia* (Cambridge, 1986), 62-70. Wright briefly mentions the lightning rod trial, 68. *The Experiments and Observations on Electricity* were translated into French by François Thomas Dalibard and published by Durand in Paris in 1752. On the French reception of Franklin's discovery, see the Abbé Nollet, *Lettre sur l'électricité* (Paris, 1753). Nollet expresses serious doubts concerning the lightning rod. M. de Romas's *Mémoire sur les moyens de se garantir de la foudre dans les maisons*, published by Bergeret at Bordeaux in 1776, reports on the author's experiments with the electric kite.

3. A. Amsterdam, 4:18. Morveau refers to two important *Mémoires* on the question. The *Mémoire* of Le Roy, published in the Collection of the Royal Academy of Sciences in 1770, and the *Mémoire* of M. de Saussure on lightning rods published in Geneva.

4. Louis Bernard, Baron Guyton de Morveau, wrote thirteen articles for the Encyclopedia. Born in Dijon in 1737, he published his *Eléments de Chimie théorique et pratique* in 1776-77. He became a member of the Legislative Assembly and later of the Convention. He sat on the Committee of Public Safety from April to July of 1793. He died in 1816. See John Lough, *The Contributors to the Encyclopédie* (London, 1973).

5. The most detailed account of this trial was given by Charles Vellay in *Annales Révolutionnaires* (January-March 1909, 25-37; April-June 1909, 201-19). See also *Causes célèbres, curieuses et intéressantes de toutes les cours souveraines du Royaume, avec les jugements qui les ont décidés* by Des Essarts (Paris, 1783), 99:3-110, and 104:125-36. Ernest Hamel, one of Robespierre's earliest biographers, speaks of the trial, although he exaggerates Robespierre's role and the fame he acquired from it. See his *Histoire de Robespierre* (Paris, 1865), 1:38-42. The historian Gérard Walter reestablishes Buissart's contribution; see *Robespierre* (Paris, 1961) 1:34-41. But Walter underestimates the friendship between Robespierre and Buissart when he accuses Robespierre of having in some way stolen the fame that should have gone to the older man. See Georges Michon's edition of the *Correspondance de Maximilien et Augustin Robespierre* (Paris, 1926).

6. Robespierre, *Oeuvres complètes* (Paris, 1952-67), 1:20.

7. Letter from M. de Vissery to Buissart, quoted in Vellay, 28.

8. Antoine-Joseph Buissart, born in Arras in 1737, was admitted to the bar in 1761 and elected to the Arras Academy in 1767. He was the king's commissioner for primary assemblies in 1790 and was elected justice of the peace in 1791. He withdrew from public life after Robespierre's execution. He was one of the most respected physicists of the city of Amiens. Cf. Vellay, 28.

9. The other side invoked in opposition to the lightning rod the opinion of two learned men, one of whom was Jean-Paul Marat. The Abbé Bertholon, himself an eminent physicist, wrote Buissart that Marat was "a crazy man who thought he could become famous by attacking many great men and producing paradoxes that seduced no one." In his *Recherches physiques sur l'électricité*, Marat wrote: "It is obvious that the fluid accumulated in clouds is beyond the

sphere of attraction of the highest conductor." He also enumerates eleven cases of conductors "blasted by lightning." Quoted by Bellay, 206-07.

10. Arras, Imprimerie de Guy Delasablionnière, in-8, 100 pages. The *Mercure de France* spoke of the trial on several occasions. In an article of June 21, 1783, it applauded the victory of science and hailed the worth of Buissart, with a flattering note on the worth of Robespierre. On May 1, 1784, the *Mercure* noted publication of Robespierre's speeches at the trial.

11. Library of the University of Pennsylvania. The letter was published for the first time in France in Vellay, 215.

12. The question of the sublime and its relation to the sacred would play an important rhetorical role in the spring of 1794, in the conceptualization both of the Cult of the Supreme Being and of the Terror. The relationship to the sublime, as that which exceeds representation, was commented on by F.A. Aulard, *Le Culte de la Raison et de l'Etre suprême* (Paris, 1892), and Jean Starobinski, *The Invention of Liberty, 1700-1789* (Geneva, 1964).

13. A.O. Aldridge speaks at length of this epigram and its success in *Franklin and his French Contemporaries* (New York, 1957), 124-42.

14. Aldridge, 128.

15. Roland Mortier, *Clartés et ombres au siècle des Lumiéres* (Geneva, 1969). See in particular 13-60.

16. Quoted in Mortier, *Clartés*, 17-21.

17. Ibid., 35. Anne Robert Jacques Turgot was an important Physiocrat and an intimate friend of Franklin's in Paris, where he was often present at the salon of Madame Helvétius. He contributed several articles to the Encyclopedia and was Comptroller General from 1774-76. On Franklin and Turgot, see also Claude-Anne Lopez, *Mon Cher Papa: Franklin and the Ladies of Paris* (New Haven, 1966), 243-71.

18. Robespierre, *Plaidoyers*, 75, 26, 28, and 71 (emphasis mine).

19. *Plaidoyers*, 27 (emphasis mine).

20. Rousseau's influence on Robespierre was considerable and is found in all the great Revolutionary speeches. It was documented at length in Carol Blum, *Rousseau and the Republic of Virtue* (Ithaca, 1984). Yet Robespierre detaches himself completely from Rousseau in his appreciation of human progress, and his conviction remains intact through his last great speeches of 1794.

21. *Plaidoyers*, 20.

22. *Ibid.*, 35 (emphasis mine).

23. *Ibid.*, 69 (emphasis mine).

24. *Ibid.*, 70.

25. *Ibid.*

26. Quoted by Ronald Paulson, *Representations of Revolution, 1789-1820* (New Haven, 1983), 44: "She also refers to 'the rumblings of the approaching tempest' and 'the gathering storm.'"

27. Ibid., 58. Paulson's analysis of the metaphors organized around the ideas of a storm, light that smashes to bits and the tempest is especially interesting here, as is all of Chapter 33, entitled "Burke, Paine and Wollstonecraft: the Sublime and the Beautiful," 57-87. In particular the idea Burke presented in 1757 in his *Philosophical Enquiry into the Origin of the Sublime and the Beautiful* is that "darkness is sublime, light is not, but extreme light, by overcoming the organs of sight, obliterates all objects, so as in its effects exactly resembles darkness" (59). See also the remark of Paulson that, for Burke, "the true sublime in government is a mixture of awe or admiration, whereas the false sublime generates only fear

and a grotesque energy" (66). Burke's views on the tragi-comic, grotesque character of the Revolution are well known; nevertheless, the concept of the sublime that Robespierre associates with the cult of the Supreme Being is not far from Burke's thought and establishes a paradoxical link between the sublime of an unchained nature, a nature that blinds and strikes dead, and the law of 22 Prairial that, following the Festival of the Supreme Being, inaugurated the Terror.

28. On the repercussions of Franklin's death in France, see Aldridge, 212-34, and expecially Gilbert Chinard, *L'Apothéose de Benjamin Franklin* (Paris, 1955).

29. Eulogy of Félix Vicq d'Azir, given before the Academy of Medicine on March 14, 1791, and reprinted in Chinard, 144-62. Félix Vicq d'Azir was a member of the Academy of Sciences and perpetual secretary of the Royal Society of Medicine. Like Robespierre and Condorcet, he died in 1794. He had been Marie-Antoinette's personal physician.

30. Condorcet, *Oeuvres*, edited by A. Condorcet O'Connor and M.F. Arago (Paris, 1847), 404.

31. *Ibid.*, 423 (emphasis mine).

32. See *Couplets civiques* for the inauguration of the busts of Franklin, Voltaire, Buffon, Jean-Jacques Rousseau, Marat and Le Pelletier, in the hall of the popular republican society of Avre-Libre, by Citizen Dourneau-Démophile, (Paris, an II).

33. This exchange between Brissot and Robespierre is discussed in the preface Monique and François Hincker wrote for their edition of Condorcet's *Des Progrès de l'esprit humain* (Paris, 1971), 58-59.

34. *Plaidoyers*, 55.

35. Condorcet, *Oeuvres*, 404.

36. Quoted by Monique and François Hincker, *Des Progrès*, 59.

37. *Ibid.*, 248.

38. *Discours et Rapports à la Convention* (Paris, 1965), 246-47. Emphasis mine. Dibutade, or Dibutades, was a legendary artist to whom (acording to Pliny) a Corinthian tradition attributed the invention of terra cotta sculpture.

39. *Ibid.*, 247.

40. *Ibid.*, 270.

41. *Ibid.*, 275.

42. *Ibid.*, 274.

43. Quoted in Aldridge, *Franklin*, 135.

44. In Chinard, *L'Apothéose*, 159.

45. *Discours et Rapports*, 125. This speech is a response to a plan for a Republic presented by Condorcet on February 15, 1793.

46. *Discours et Rapports*, 265; May 7, 1794.

47. On Condorcet's death, see the chapter Michelet devotes to him in his *Histoire de la Révolution Francaise* (Paris, 2:815-21), as well as Gérard Walter's corrections in the appendix, 1304. After being declared subject to arrest, Condorcet hid for a time in Paris, then left the city on March 25, 1794. It was only after 9 Thermidor that Madame Condorcet instituted inquiries about a man who starved to death and was found in the Meudon forest. See Barroux, "A propos de la mort de Condorcet" in *Révolution française*, 69:1916. See also Elizabeth and Robert Badinter, *Condorcet, un intellectuel en politique* (Paris, 1988).

48. D.A.F. de Sade, *Français, encore un effort* (Paris, 1965), 35-36. In his introduction entitled "L'Inconvenance majeure," Maurice Blanchot compares certain texts by Saint-Just and Sade. He stresses in particular the idea of Sade that

"a new republic will have the means to survive by its virtues, but an already old and corrupted nation will be able to preserve itself only by many crimes." It must be added that this idea comes straight from the formulation of the political state given by Rousseau in the *Discours sur l'Origine de l'inégalité*, where he notes, "The political state will remain forever imperfect, for it was almost the work of chance and, since it was badly begun, time, while uncovering its flaws and suggesting remedies, could never repair the vices of its constitution." *Oeuvres complètes* (Paris, 1966), 3:180.

49. *Les Infortunes de la Vertu* (Paris, 1968), 185.

50. *Justine*, trans. Richard Seaver and Austryn Wainhouse (New York, 1966), 742. The first version of *Justine, Les Infortunes de la Vertu*, was probably written in 1787. It was discovered and published in 1930. *Justine ou les malheurs de la Vertu* dates from 1791. The third version, *La Nouvelle Justine*, comes from 1797. Justine does not die at the end but becomes the audience of the *Histoire de Juliette*; the prosperity of vice functions as a metaphoric thunderbolt.

51. *Ibid.* This passage, taken from the *Infortunes de la Vertu*, also serves as the novel's epigraph.

52. *Français, encore un effort*, 75 (emphasis mine).

53. *Ibid.*, 72.

54. *Ibid.*, 77.

55. Blanchot, "L'Inconvenance majeure," 37.

56. *Ibid.*

57. *Français, encore un effort*, 81.

WORDS OF CHANGE: AUGUST 12, 1789

Christie McDonald

More than any other single event, the French Revolution lays before the amateur and professional of history, the reader of texts and the dreamer, the question of how change comes about in society. As a crisis, it was the event through which society marked at once its rupture with and affiliation to the past. As the promise of "new" society, the Revolution provided a remarkable example of how a hierarchical system transformed itself by inventing a theory and practice of egalitarianism. Extending from 1789 through 1794, the Revolution delineates a special period, an origin of sorts, itself distinct from that which preceded and followed it, and creates a before and after. Something dies in 1789: the French Monarchy. And something is born: the idea of a Republic. Before, there is feudalism and nobility; after, capitalism and the bourgeoisie. As one of the most dramatic events in recent history, the French Revolution is not merely co-extensive with the beginning of the republic; it is a promise of equality and a privileged form of change.[1]

Given the goals of democracy, and the difficulty of measuring the distance between the achievements and intentions of the Revolution, the question is what began and who changed during the summer of 1789? That this question is, despite its apparent simplicity, mined is not surprising. Not only because of the complexity of events during the summer of 1789, but because a working concept of what revolution means, as well as a sense of how to interpret the "facts" and "events" of history, is needed even to begin to answer it.

The modern concept of revolution involves a narrative of beginnings, a story in which, as Hanna Arendt put it, "the course of history suddenly begins anew . . . an entirely new story, a story never known or told before."[2] The revolutionary calendar, for example, launched a new history, marking year one at the king's fall from kingship. But what underlies any "new" story of such dramatic proportions are the coincident notions of a beginning and a first principle (here freedom and invention), a subject of reflection since the time of Plato. In his book, François Furet criticizes the general concept of revolution, as he eloquently

unpacks the French Revolution. Recognizing that most historiography reproduces the contours of its object, Furet asks for
something else: a new historiography, one that takes a critical
distance in order to re-evaluate both the past and the present.
Furet presents the Revolution as both the model and question for
such an investigation.[3] There is no "fact" of the French
Revolution that stands objectively in the comprehension of all,
though few would dispute that this sequence of events, however
interpreted, changed the political and social landscape of Europe
from 1789 on.

As a political event, the Revolution marked a new beginning,
but it was nevertheless prepared by the philosophers of the
Enlightenment, an era "Peter Gay summed up in two words:
"criticism and power."[4] The critical spirit of classical thought
spurred thinkers of the eighteenth century to question the
Christian underpinnings of their tradition, with the result that
Greco-Roman antiquity offered a plausible intellectual alternative
to the onto-theological tradition. At the same time, those thinkers
worked through the contemporary issue of power. Towards the
mid-eighteenth century, the word revolution began to signify a
positive ideal and political transformation.[5] With the Enlightenment the term came to be viewed as, first, an event and, then, a
new form of discourse that would institute the means of political
and social action.

The creation of terms connected with the Revolution has often
been explained by the transference of religious vocabulary onto
the events and documents of political action. Critics cite
Mirabeau who called the National Assembly "the *inviolable
priesthood* of national policy,"[6] and stated that "The Declaration
of Rights ha[d] become a *political gospel* and the French
constitution a *religion* for which the people . . . [were] ready to
die."[7] Others point out that the sequence of events in 1789 made
this vocabulary believable. But the Revolution was more than a
political arena in which religious ideas were secularized. It was a
dramatization in the strongest sense of the term, an experiment in
the political concept of democracy as a national ideology.
However much eighteenth-century thought prepared the way—
and here is the paradox—the Revolution was an invention
without precedent, the consequences of which were to be
staggering throughout the centuries to follow. In the name of
fraternity, equality and liberty, the people were to justify political
action in order to break down the resistance of those considered
to be enemies and wipe out the past.[8]

I wish to focus on the following question: were there moments in the Revolution that constituted absolute starting points for universal principles? And if there were, how did they manifest themselves? In particular, what was the relationship between word and act, violence and innovation? In order to give a brief and very partial response, I will analyse one event: a narrative account of a given day at the National Assembly, August 12, 1789, when, at the Assembly's request and in a landmark speech, Guy-Jean-Baptiste Target is to inform the King of recent events. I will argue that language in the National Assembly performs a collective annihilation of the individual at the very moment when the Assembly purports to celebrate individual rights. In this way, the National Assembly both repeats the past and innovates when in August 1789 it performs the substitution of its own civil right for that of the nobility—in the creation of a "new" authoritative body and a rhetorical lesson of social power and truth. Through a series of discrete linguistic acts, society founds the general principles of what will become the nation.

The account with which I will deal was written by Heinrich Campe, an innocent bystander to the events at the National Assembly on August 12, 1789. In order to situate this narrative in the context of that fateful summer, one must keep in mind the sequence of events. On May 5, the States-General met at Versailles for the first time since 1614; the reason was fiscal reform. The astonishing acts had only begun. On June 17, the Third Estate named itself the National Assembly which, closed out of the Hôtel des Menus-Plaisirs, met on June 20 and pledged not to disband until a constitution was put in place. On June 27, the king legalized the National Assembly. The events of the summer move quickly, and violence begins: on July 14 the Bastille is taken; in August the "great fear" dominates throughout the countryside; on the night of August 4, the nobles and clergy of the Assembly change the course of history by joyously relinquishing their privileges. That they do so by converting feudal rights into bourgeois capital and proclaiming Louis XVI the "restorer of French liberty" is almost insignificant next to the historic gesture of creating a new order. Several days later, on August 11, the Assembly votes in the decree abolishing the feudal structure, an act annihilating almost the entire social system of the *ancien régime*.

It is this extraordinary act that sets the stage for what occurs on August 12. The story is that of Joachim Heinrich Campe, a German, become a French citizen by decree of the National

Assembly; he finds himself in the position of spectator to the events of the Assembly on August 12, 1789. What follows is a synopsis of his most remarkable account.

Campe moves towards the room where the meeting of the National Assembly is being held; there he is told that the room is full and no one else may enter. At this very moment, one of the deputies from the nobility happens into the hall. The narrator addresses him, explaining that he has come at the invitation of Count Mirabeau and wishes the deputy to inform Mirabeau of his arrival. *De tout coeur* responds the deputy warmly. As he is escorted to his seat by Mirabeau, the narrator feels deep respect for the dignity of the meeting, a feeling that will be very short-lived.

In the room, the atmosphere is tumultuous: confused sounds come from all sides, some in polyphony, others in cacophony. For ten full minutes the narrator cannot grasp in the least what is happening around him. Ringing his bell, the chairman insistently yells "Order." While some of the members attempt to gain silence, others struggle to deliver speeches; all fail. Although the people in the room and gallery seem to understand the proceedings, the narrator finds the whole scene unintelligible. He likens his ears to the eyes of one who, emerging from darkness into light, feels blinded: slowly, he begins to distinguish the principal from the secondary voices and comprehends a few phrases.

Then, Campe describes how two parish priests are prevented from speaking as they attempt to address the Assembly with a speech and text respectively; it is unclear whether the protest is over the priests' proposals or the manner in which they present them. Cries of *En poche! En poche! A bas! A bas!* express discontent from the group right up until the two leave the platform. Again, several deputies struggle to speak; only the most stentorian raise their voices above the tumult, although they too are interrupted at almost every phrase by sounds of approval or disapproval, applause or laughter. With fists raised and face muscles tensed in anger, a few very athletic orators manage to glare down the disrupters; they force the attention of the chaotic Assembly through a quasi-physical struggle.

When a matter of real importance comes up, however, the Assembly grinds to utter silence. Such a moment comes with the address by Guy-Jean-Baptiste Target, an academic lawyer. It is a momentous occasion: the Assembly has requested the presence of the king to celebrate a *Te Deum* upon the "completion" of the Revolution. Having divested itself of feudal rights only a few days earlier, the Assembly will bestow the title "restorer of French liberty" upon Louis XVI to inaugurate the new world of egalitarianism. The tone of this speech, the *first* address of the liberated nation to its king, will set a precedent for all future addresses of this kind.

The drop of a pin could have been heard in the chapel.

Not for long, however.

Target, it seems, forgets that he no longer writes or speaks in the name of an obsequious academy, but now in the name of a liberated people. So that when he begins, the reaction is thunderous:

Target: *Sire, the National Assembly has the honor . . .*

Voices roar: *No honor no honor, strike this word.*

Target: *Sire, the National Assembly has the honor of putting at Your Majesty's feet . . .*

The walls and windows shake from the hullabaloo. Voices: *Down with feet! Down with feet.*

A voice penetrates through: *The National Assembly puts nothing at the feet of anyone.*

Target, beginning again: *Sire, the National Assembly brings to Your Majesty . . .*

Voices: *Bravo.*

Target: *Brings the offering to Your Majesty.*

Pandemonium. Mirabeau: *One can only use the word offering when addressing either God or an idol; the king is neither of these.*

The Assembly finds Target's next sentence too long, too verbose, after which he is forced off the platform to modify his address. He returns fifteen minutes later, but the response is the same. The Assembly criticizes and rejects each sentence with equal violence. Mirabeau picks up on the word drunkenness (*ivresse*): *Gentlemen, the legislative body can be neither drunk nor tipsy.* Applause and laughter from all corners. For the second time, Target is forced off the platform.

The narrator comments that although he himself is a pedagogue and had heard and given many a correction in school exercises, he had still never witnessed such an implacable critique. He likens Target to a schoolboy who, desperate and ashamed, brings wretchedly bad homework to his teacher. What more could he do?

Back for the third time, Target remains below the platform. He stands on the rostrum in front of a large table. His corrected address now seems as simple as anyone could wish, and the Assembly finds little with which to reproach him.[9]

In the narrative of this scene, the National Assembly dramatizes a "democratization" of language. The voices of the multitude shout down a single voice invested with the values of the past, forcing Target to suppress certain words no longer acceptable: honor, feet, offering, drunkenness. At stake throughout this account are the changing codes and conventions in language of which the main character seems oblivious: whence the humor. As a laboratory for the regeneration of society, however, the consequences of such action will become lethal. Target errs here not only because he can't quite get anything right, but also because change is occurring simultaneously with the pronunciation of the words. By the exclusion of these words, rendered unacceptable because of change, the Assembly performs a lesson to one of its members, and institutes a social order in which individual will must be subsumed into the will of the collectivity. That this does not occur through the free action of the individual, in the person of Target, foreshadows at a linguistic level the violence that will later erupt empirically from these paradoxes. *In its first day of conventional quality, the Assembly puts four words to death.*

The Assembly creates a new truth whose foundation and even verification must be found in its own acts.[10] Truth value resides in the principle of the collective will, which becomes co-extensve with experimentation of its force. As a precedent for the Revolution, what does this mean? It means, first, that the rhetoric of the *ancien régime* will be subjected to the power of the many in the abolition of one language and the creation of another. It means, further, that the right to invention through language will be regulated by norms no less authoritarian than those preceding 1789. Five days after this account, the Assembly deliberates on a Declaration of Rights.[11] It would seem then that at the very moment the Assembly is preparing a Declaration of Rights *de jure* which will precede the creation of the constitution, those rights *de facto* are being denied. Simple causal explanations, however, do not suffice. Reinventing the social order in the "person" of the "people," and particularly in the concept of the "nation," requires a fiction, a collective fiction that would impose itself as the new "reality."

More than a sequence of actions, the Revolution not only depended upon but was a language, a language of consensus through which men and women spoke.[12] The form through which this consensus was achieved was presumed to be a dialogue. But the principle upon which this dialogue was based could not be that of rational discourse directed at rationality.[13]

The rhetorical lesson of this narrative may be interpreted positively as the force of eloquence and passion inventing the language of the Revolution. The right of the Assembly to deny individual rights of speech, *as a precedent*, would appear then to confirm that passion (for equality and country) comes first in effecting change; and reason acts only in the service of passion. Yet any simple confirmation of this sort counters the explicit impetus given prior to and concomitant with the beginning of the Revolution: action must and should be justified in the name of reason as a way to further the social progress of humanity. One of the explicit goals of the vast project of the *Encyclopedia*, as an expression of collective eighteenth-century thought, under the direction of Denis Diderot, was to "change the way in which men [and women] think." Passion in the service of reason, not the reverse, was a view aptly summed up by Mme de Stáel: *"Since new thoughts develop new feelings, the progress of philosophy must provide new means for eloquence."*[14] Both reason and passion were considered the "natural" links of a republican association; the question was which was to dominate and how. And, in the long term, as Kant would later phrase it, was progress for the better?

The collective answer would had to have been yes, in the name of reason, although singular voices might have been more circumspect. The scene described by Campe combines the two elements that, though they may seem contradictory, make up what Hanna Arendt calls "the spirit of revolution": the act of foundation, involving the need for stabilization, and the thrill of bringing something new into being.[15] The narrator of our story, a German teacher, presents the Assembly as the first collective pedagogue of the nation. The collective teacher edits the address of one of its members, founding change upon a principle of naming. At the same time, the Assembly dramatizes the need for public instruction to alter the habits of the people. It is a first step in the direction of public instruction, the model for which would not be set up until 1791. Shortly after the troubled summer of 1789, public instruction would come to be viewed as a mechanism by which to stabilize the rocky and fragile institutions of the new society. It was to be based on reason and the sense that in an enlightened nation the people could not and would not allow themselves to be enslaved. In other words, the development of a system of education and instruction would guarantee the freedom of the individual within the system.

The *precedent* of this impromptu inaugural lesson in Campe's account coincides at one level with the principles of the future educational system: the student and citizen must to be at one with the goals of democracy. But at another level, it violates the very principles it founds: as creator and teacher of both equality and "equal opportunity," the Assembly brings about change in language through censorship. Change cannot be equated here with individual freedom to choose it, for change comes about through force. Target is not allowed freedom of speech. That he has not liberated his language from its former models in the tradition does not justify in principle the newly empowered Assembly to fall back on former patterns of authority through force. From this single event, it seems clear that change occurs through a complex combination of repetition and innovation. It seems clear also that even the concept of change, understood as a beginning and a principle, became part of a vocabulary-in-the-making during the summer of 1789. By staking out a language for itself and disallowing eloquent variation from the past, this lesson by the Assembly marks a precedent in language control that might have given pause to the emergent leaders of the Revolution. As the Assembly proclaims these "new" feelings and thoughts through the forcible change of words, they are in danger of repeating the inherited patterns they wish to destroy. That is, by denying the right of the individual (word), such a totalizing form of "egalitarianism" may (and did in fact later) reinstate factionalism in a form all the more chaotic and explicitly violent because society was no longer stabilized by a fixed hierarchy.

The need to name and rename as events unfolded (to rewrite history through names and naming) demonstrates to what extent rhetoric became a measure of mastery and control; and the changes in language, as the account of August 12 shows, were no more pacific than the political changes that accompanied them. As a recent critic has written: "One of the most telling symptoms of the weakening of the Marxist paradigm in the study of the French Revolution is the growing interest . . . in the political vocabulary of the French Revolution not as mere rhetoric . . . but as a means of transforming the symbolic grounding of the national community, the supremely political act of redefining the body politic."[16] Rhetoric, that is, not only communicated change but was the condition of possibility for change to happen.

What then is new in 1789? If the name of the break with the *ancien régime* was revolution, the name of that form of government being invented was *democracy*. Although the term "democracy," like "aristocracy" and "monarchy," goes back to Aristotle (all were common terms of political thinkers in the Middle Ages), it was almost never used positively prior to the Revolution in France; the words "democrat" and "aristocrat" only came into usage at the very end of the *ancien régime*. When the terms were coined, they did not indicate adherence to a membership in a group or class of people. Rather, a democrat was one who believed in a democratic society.[17]

The creation of a democratic state is at some level synonymous with the philosophical ideal of the *ancien régime*. The Revolution reclaims this ideal by renaming it and *believing* that it has invented democracy: change not so much in the intellectual and political order, but change in the perception of who and what has created it for the contemporaries as well as the generations to follow.[18] What is the relationship of the intellectuals who preceded the Revolution to the institutions that followed? Did these intellectuals prepare and provoke the Revolution? Tocqueville's thesis had been that the role of the intellectuals in French society was assumed by *default:* in search of leadership and the means of representation which did not exist, the body politic would only follow the intellectuals when they lacked their own delegates.[19] Cochin's analysis is more original: the philosophers do not invent by default; they are not substitutes for politicians; they embody political democracy in its quintessential, abstract form.[20]

There are two types of democracy. The first is "corporative," the kind put forth by the *ancien régime* in which power comes out of and is addressed to a nation constituted of bodies. In this type of democracy, no structural change occurs: hierarchies and rights, leaders and diverse values remain. In the second type of democracy society is transformed into an abstraction of equal individuals, no matter what their background or social milieu; only the vote makes the individual into a political entity. Because the people as an abstract principle cannot act, this kind of democracy necessitates a special field called politics, bringing with it politicians, parties and ideologies. Mediation through representation becomes a *sine qua non* of democracy. However, representative democracy was not the ideal of pure democracy that the philosophers had conceived.

Pure democracy was to be the will of the people turned into law. As such, it distinguishes the rule of the many from the concept of the general will. The dream of transparency, summed up in Rousseau's notion of the general will, went further than voluntary or conscious choice to agree; it bound the individual to the totality: "The general will alone can guide the forces of the State according to the end for which it was instituted, which is the common good.... Since the will always tends toward the good of the being who wills, since the private will always has as its object private interest and the general will common interest, it follows that this last alone is or ought to be the true motivation of the social body."[21] Based on a view of the "truth" of man's and woman's nature, this vision of society maintains the freedom of the individual, encapsulated in abstract equality, within a collectivity without delegates or leaders. It was an impossible ideal, as Rousseau already knew before he wrote the *Social Contract*. The fiction in his novel *La Nouvelle Héloïse* shows the disintegration of the general will within the imagined society of Clarens based on a logic of the individual character of Julie.[22] That is, the novel tells the story of how, in a society aspiring to transparent democracy, the power must be hidden elsewhere.

This was the very pitfall that Mirabeau sought to avoid by naming the delegates to the National Assembly *representatives of the French people* [*représentants du peuple français*]. On June 16, 1789, he summed up what he saw as the consensus of the members: "It is the work of this Assembly, and the work of this Assembly alone, to interpret and present the general will of the nation."[23] Indivisible in its mission as in its activity, immune to veto power by the individual factions, the Assembly was to be a synecdoche for the nation. But those opposed to Mirabeau maintained that the word "people" signified at once too much and too little. Defined according to the Latin *populus*, it means nation, a goal more general than that of the assembly at the time; defined according to the Latin word *plebs*, it supposes orders and differences among the orders: just what the assembly wished to prevent. Some feared that the word could mean what the Latins called *vulgus*, what the English called *mob*, and what aristocrats and commoners alike called *canaille*.[24]

On June 15, 1789, Mirabeau proposed that the representatives no longer be those of any individual state, class or profession, but that they be those of the French People. "I adopt it, I defend it, I proclaim it, in the name of reason which makes it [the expression] right."[25] It is the freedom to choose this performative that so exhilarates Mirabeau and those around him, the freedom to will the ideal of a nation into being. The conferral of the new title is the first step in fusing the people and their representatives into wholeness.

When Mirabeau presents the project for the Declaration of Rights to the National Assembly on August 17, 1789, he speaks in Cartesian terms. Illuminated by a sense of reason, he states that a Declaration of Rights that responded to an ideal of perfection would contain axioms so simple, evident and rich in impact that to deviate from them would appear absurd; such a declaration should be the keystone from which all constitutions emanate. At the same time, a declaration is not an abstract philosophical tract, based on deductive reason. A Declaration of Rights must come out of and lead back to *everyday experience.* He declares that abstract terms are necessary; they must be made intelligible by their relationship to those "sensations from which liberty was born."[26]

The account of August 12 at the National Assembly brings into vivid relief the distance between the ideal of totality and indivisibility and the actual state of language and affairs. Having extravagantly thrown their privileges to the wind, the nobility, along with the clergy and Third Estate, must live out the effects of the newly formed "general will." Unlike Francis Coppola's revival of silent film in his *Napoleon,* which makes action and power visual, the power of the National Assembly to transform the world comes first through words: the power to suppress, change and name. Rousseau had prepared the way when he wrote that the first social institution was language,[27] and he understood that to change society would require turning the arms of the institution against itself.

But did society change overnight? The answer is yes and no. On August 11, the Assembly votes in the decree abolishing the feudal structure. On August 12, an aggregate of individuals shouts down Target, deleting the words "honor," "feet" and "offering." The problem was one of passing from contiguity, in the will of the many, to continuity, in the consensus of the collectivity—a problem that Denis Diderot had confronted in articulating his brand of scientific materialism. Moreover, the account of one event, among these first experiments in democracy, demonstrated that to change individual words in a particular context did not necessarily change the system of language. Nor did isolated individual action necessarily bring about social regeneration.

The rhetorical lesson of August 12, 1789, as subsequent events would bear out, showed that traditional society, founded on inequality, would clash with the new society, founded on an ideal of egalitarianism and a tenuous if not imaginary consensus. Out of this conflict would come change, both pacific and violent, welcome and repulsed. In the scene recounted above, the National Assembly plays the role of demagogue in both of its accepted meanings: in the ancient sense in which a popular orator-leader takes on the cause of the people against other factions in the state; and in the newer, pejorative sense in which the leader of a faction or unruly group reaches out to the passions of the mob. Despite usage dating back to the fifteenth century, demagogue was only accepted by the Academy in 1762, the year in which Rousseau's *Social Contract* appeared. Although the National Assembly was drunk with the rejection of honor to the king, offered in the name of equality, its real *feat* was to bring leadership of and through the people: a democratic performance.

NOTES

1. François Furet, *Penser la Révolution française* (Paris 1978), 18. In English, see *Interpreting the French Revolution* (Cambridge, Eng., 1981). This view constitutes a critique of the Marxian view of the Revolution as the historical necessity of class struggle: the rise of the bourgeois class to power. On questions of ideology, intellectual history and the Revolution, see Keith Michael Baker, "On the Problem of the Ideological Origins of the French Revolution," *Modern European Intellectual History: Reappraisals and New Perspectives*, ed. Dominick Lacapra and Steven L. Kaplan (Ithaca, N.Y., 1985), 197-220.

2. Hanna Arendt, *On Revolution* (Middlesex, 1963), 28.

3. See Furet, *Penser*, 46.

4. Peter Gay, *The Enlightenment: An Interpretation.* (New York, 1967), xi.

5. It was in Germany that the sense of revolution as a wide and radical change, beyond any particular political event, became instituted. Frederick the Great became interested in revolution as both political and social event, and his influence was felt by the Germans. The writers of the *Sturm und Drang* took up the issues he raised through his reforms and impatience with tradition. Mirabeau brought the concept to France; in a study of Frederick the Great in 1788, he described Prussia as the locus of a coming revolution. Then, in his speeches and discourses during the following year, he transferred what he had learned in Germany to hopes for France. He was the first to coin the terms "counter revolution," "counter-revolutionary," and "anti-revolutionary"; see James Billington, *Fire in the Minds of Men* (New York, 1980),p. 20. It is said that the night the

Bastille was taken, Louis XVI queried, "Is it a riot?" to which the Duke of Liancourt responded: "Non, Sire, it is a *revolution*" (Ferdinand Brunot, *Histoire de la langue française* [Paris, 1937], 9:617).

6. Cited in Billington, *Fire*, 20.

7. "La Déclaration des Droits est devenue un *évangile politique* pour laquelle le peuple est prêt à périr." Letter from Roland to the King, 10 juin 1792, Buchez et Roux, *Histoire de la Révolution française ou journal des Assemblées Nationales* (Paris, 1834), 15.42; cited in Brunot, 624.

8. Furet, *Penser*, 51.

9. Gerald Walter, "Un allemand à Paris au lendemain du 4 août: impressions de voyage de Joachim Heinrich Campe, pédegogue allemand, devenu citoyen française par décret de l'assemblée nationale," *La révolution française*, in *Mémoriales du siècle* (Paris, 1967).

10. Put in the terms of J.L. Austin, in *How to do Things with Words*, this situation exemplifies the assimilation of the constative (a statement whose truth conditions are verifiable) to the performative (the performing of an action) that Sandy Petrey has forcefully argued in a lecture entitled "Performance et subjectivité chez Balzac."

11. François Furet et Denis Richet, *La Révolution française* (Paris, 1965), 89.

12. Furet, *Penser*, 279.

13. I have argued elsewhere that both Rousseau and Diderot contested the limitation of philosophic dialogue to rational discourse. Dialogue in this pre-revolutionary context is both a dialectical method designed to reveal truth and the performance of that method. See *The Dialogue of Writing* (Waterloo, 1985).

14. "L'éloquence appartenant plus aux sentiments qu'aux idées, paraît moins susceptible que la philosophie de progrès indéfinis. Cependant, *comme les pensées nouvelles développent de nouveaux sentiments, les progrès de la philosophie doivent fournir à l'éloquence de nouveaux moyens.*" Madame de Staël, *De la littérature*, critical edition by Paul Van Tieghem (Geneva, 1958), 2:413.

15. "To the extent that the greatest event in every revolution is the act of foundation, the spirit of revolution contains two elements which to us seem irreconcilable and even contradictory. The act of founding the new body politic, of devising the new form of government involves the grave concern with the stability and durability of the new structure; the experience, on the other hand, which those who are engaged in this grave business are bound to have is the exhilarating awareness of the human capacity of beginning, the high spirits which have always attended the birth of something new on earth" (Arendt, 222-223).

16. Baker, in *Modern European Intellectual History*, 204.

17. See R.R. Palmer, "Notes on the Use of the Word Democracy," *The Political Science Quarterly* (1953), 68:203-226. Palmer points out that even in America, "democracy" and "democrat" did not always take on a positive connotation; "in America . . . as far as they had any currency at all, [they] were foisted by the conservatives upon sympathizers with the revolution—that is they were terms of abuse or reproach, smear-words, used to discredit people who would not use them of themselves" (*Ibid.*, 207). In Europe, "democracy" was first used in a favorable sense in Belgium, and was not often used in the early years of the French Revolution. Robespierre's speech in the Convention on February 5, 1794, is the one most often referred to: "It is time to mark clearly the aim of the Revolution . . . Only democratic or republican government; these two words are

synonymous, despite the abuse of popular language, for aristocracy is no more the republic than monarchy is . . . Democracy is a state in which the people, as sovereign, guided by laws of its own making, does for itself all that it can do well, and by its delegates what it cannot . . . The French are the first people in the world to establish a true democracy, by calling all men to enjoy equality and the fullness of civic rights; and that, in my opinion, is the real reason why all the tyrants allied against the Republic will be defeated." *Moniteur*, February 7, 1894; see also C. Vellay, *Discours et rapports de Robespierre* (Paris, 1908), 324-328. Cited in Palmer, 214-215. Palmer reminds the reader that this association of democracy with Robespierre tended then to discredit the term since he was associated with terror and "judicial murder."

18. Furet, *Penser*, 274.

19. Ibid., 282.

20. Ibid.

21. Jean-Jacques Rousseau, "Geneva Manuscript," *On the Social Contract*, ed. Roger Masters, trans. Judith Masters (New York, 1978), 167. See also 59-61 for the passages on the general will in the final version of the *Social Contract* which are not as explicit as this formulation. The answer was a social contract based on the general will: "Each of us puts his person and all his power in common under the supreme direction of the general will; and in a body we receive each member as an indivisible part of the whole" (53).

22. I have argued this elsewhere in *The Extravagant Shepherd*, in *Studies on Voltaire and the Eighteeneth Century* (Banbury, 1973).

23. "Il appartient à cette assemblée, il n'appartient qu'à elle d'interpréter et de présenter la volonté générale de la nation" (Mirabeau, *Discours et opinions* [Paris, 1820], 1:200).

24. Ibid., 1:202.

25. Ibid., 1:203.

26. "S'il faut employer des termes abstraits, nous les rendrons intelligibles en les liant à tout ce qui peut rappeler les sensations qui ont servi à faire éclore la liberté, et en écartant, autant qu'il est possible, tout ce qui se présente sous l'appareil de l'innovation" (*Opinions et discours de Mirabeau* [Paris, 1820], 2:302).

27. On the *Essay on the Origin of Languages* in *On the Origin of Languages* (New York, 1966), 5.

"ARISTOCRATE," "ARISTOCRATIE": LANGUAGE AND POLITICS IN THE FRENCH REVOLUTION

Patrice Higonnet

"The goal of the political order," wrote Sieyes in an unpublished note, "is individual liberty, the private weal [la chose privée]." For "the mole of the French Revolution"—to use Robespierre's expression—entrepreneurialism, that is to say individualism in economic life, lies embedded in nature and in reason. Roberto Zapperi has correctly identified Sieyes as an avid reader of Adam Smith and an early apologist for the division of labor. Without doubt, the author of *What is the Third Estate?* can be seen as both the archetypal representative of the French revolutionary bourgeoisie and as the harbinger also of industrial capitalism. Quite representatively, however, Sieyes was no mere Lockean, but a feminist as well, and a nationalist, hostile to the exclusion of the poor from the franchise. "In whatever way a nation wills," he wrote, "it suffices that it wills; all forms are good, and its will is always the supreme law." Sieyes, a national universalist, as it were, imagined "the law at the center of a huge globe: all citizens without exception stand at the same distance on the circumference; all depend on the law, all offer it their liberty, and property to protect; and that is what I call the common rights of the citizens in which they are all alike"[1]

Sieyes's priorities serve here as a short-hand notation for the central aporia of the French Revolution, a contradiction which was for the young Marx (as it is for us) the hermeneutic key for a reading of the revolutionary drama. In the jacobinized and revolutionary state, the distant limits of heroic (and masculinist) individualism must become contiguous with those of civic virtue and fraternity. The French Revolution may have "made the bourgeoisie mistress of the world," as Lefebvre suggested, by clearing the institutional decks of Europe for entrepreneurial capitalism, but this unfolding was—to put it mildly—a ruse of history. The Jacobin abominates "egoism." Robespierre's hatred of bankers is well known. It took some time for the audience of Jacobin ideology to apprehend that "the realm of Reason" would have to take shape as the more limited "realm of the

47

bourgeoisie." As Marc Richir has quipped insightfully, it is the French Revolution that made the bourgeoisie rather than the bourgeoisie which made the Revolution.[2]

The fragile and unstable union of individualism and communitarian values in Revolutionary consciousness finds its most obvious linguistic expression in the term *patriote*. Potentially more revealing, however—and the subject of this essay— is the linguistic antithesis of the *patriote*, the fabled *aristocrate*. Here was the choicest weapon in the Revolutionary's linguistic armory. More than any other term, this word enabled the Jacobin to ignore the relentlessly widening conflicts encrusted in his own beliefs.

In revolutionary usage, a *patriote* harmonizes within his life and thought the antinomies of *l'esprit Révolutionnaire*. He is a hero who successfully collapses the public and the private. He realizes his subjectivity in the limitless cult of civic virtue. He empowers his individuality in the collective. His redemptive breviary is the ethico-political system adumbrated by Sieyes. All Revolutionary families of thought, it may be added, from the Fayettists to the Girondins, shared this sensibility whose essence was *L'esprit révolutionnaire*. "La Révolution est un bloc." The task of the Jacobins was merely to refine this common message, to make of it the language of the Convention and the clubs, to extract from this vague sensibility a lucidly articulated and irresistible ideology whose power had less to do with the numbers of its practitioners than with its own strength and logic. Like the Feuillants, like Barnave in his *première manière*, the advanced Jacobin (albeit more militantly) silences the enemies of humanity. He educates the unknowing ones whose inner thoughts and unformulated needs find their best expression in his own voice. He is a committed nationalist. Sincere and selfless, he abominates the vicious, "anational," and egoistic *aristocrate*, who is his perfect antithesis.

The *aristocrate* is the particularist enemy of the Revolutionary spirit. He is often an *émigré* who has knowingly rejected fraternity and liberty. Thriving on the demonic and selfish side of man, he is a parasite, incapable of virile self-assertion. The fear of aristocracy, as a collective phenomenon, manifests itself in the deep concern for the aristocratic plot, a revolutionary obsession whose exaggeration has struck historians as divergent in their views as Georges Lefebvre and François Furet. The practical effect of the aristocrat's supposed existence is obvious: if aristocracy exists, patriotism must also be real. The hatred of aristocracy strengthens the resolve of the patriot and gives substance to his warnings. More tangibly, the machinations of aristocracy provide a standing category of criminality that allows the judicial exclusion of opponents, first of the right, but eventually of the left as well. As *aristocratie* acquired verbal consistency and was enmeshed in a web of moral and physical attributes, an artifact of language became a fact of politics. Though never a legal offense as such, aristocracy became a rhetorical category of criminality for which tangible proof could easily be secured.

Constitutive terms like Liberty, Equality, People, or Nation generate the ideological structures of *l'esprit révolutionnaire*. By contrast, *aristocratie* is only a negative concept. Nonetheless, its myriad uses did enable the revolutionaries to create a coherent semantic map for political action. The word *aristocrate* does not create the Revolution, but it makes it politically possible.

1

Before 1789, and more precisely until the last months of 1788, the term *aristocrate* did not appear fated to a spectacular unfolding. It was familiar only to readers of political science and was not necessarily pejorative. Rousseau had explained that "Government may . . . be restricted to a small number, so that the total of simple members exceeds that of its magistrates. This form goes by the name *aristocracy* . . . It is the best and most natural arrangement that . . . the wise should govern the masses, provided that they govern them always for their good, and not selfishly."[3]

In the late 1780's, however, the term began to evolve. Though still taken to mean the rule of the few, it also took on an elitist and negative connotation. Brissot, in 1782 a friend and defender of Marat then embroiled in the phlogiston debate, considered that in the "empire of science" both despotism and aristocrats were intolerable.[4] The social coloring of this elitist undercurrent had a nuanced effect, since it now enabled modernising observers to distinguish between "[la] noblesse antique et respectable, dont l'origine se perd dans la nuit des temps"[5] and the more elitist and tyrannical "aristocrates féodaux."[6] Of these, the Parliamentary nobility were invariably thought to be the worst. Even Lamoignon, a minister of the king, accused the parlementaires of being "une aristocratie de magistrats."[7]

The Revolution accelerated the mutation of what was meant by *aristocratie*. Once a social or learned term, the term was rapidly politicized. On June 16, 1789, Mirabeau denounced "les aristocrates, tant nobles que roturiers qui traitent le peuple de canaille."[8] Here was (to my knowledge) the first revolutionary reference to non-noble *aristocrates*, and this new usage soon became so common that after 1791 that nobles were left behind as a trivial social subset of an *aristocratie* that was otherwise defined. Hence the need to coin rather awkward terms like the "aristrocratie des ex-nobles," "aristocratie nobiliaire et équestre," or even "aristocratie ci-devant nobiliaire." (By contrast, the term "ci-devant aristocrate" is never to be found, an indirect indication of the extent to which the moralizing and political definition of the term had crowded out its purely social variant.) We can also briefly note in passing that the application of the term *aristocrate* to anti-revolutionary non-nobles of all kinds did not do the ci-devant second estate much good because it soon became quite clear—to the Jacobins at least—that all nobles were selfish, if not by birth at least by habit. Not all aristocrats were nobles, to be sure, but all nobles were for various reasons more or less *aristocrates*. Rivarol mocked this shift in meaning: "Is it not derisive to label as *aristocrats* poor noblemen . . . who might die in debtor's prison for being unable to clear a debt of one hundred écus. What must the magistrates of Bern and the nobles of Venice think of the Parisians' ignorance which has made of their governance not just an insult but a hanging offense."[9] Many liberal nobles tried to disengage themselves from this morass: after the king's flight to Varennes in June 1791, the marquis de Ferrieres explained for example that he stood apart from both the "aristocrates et . . . [les] courtisans."[10] To no avail: in June 1791, one of Marat's correspondents could write that "tous les officiers ci-devant nobles sont aristocrates."[11]

What was lost in social space was regained in historical time. True, in a universalised polity where all citizens had been *régénérés par la liberté*, birth was no longer admissible as cause for the exclusion of any French*men*, be they Jews or nobles. However, it was now compensationally possible to identify as *aristocrates* all those who had throughout History been incapable of reconciling their private ambitions to some transcendental public goal. In a note attached to his play *Socrates*, Collot d'Herbois explained that the word was etymologically linked not to government by the best, but to "arès, qui veut dire fer . . . Par *Aristocratie* les Athéniens entendoient *la contrainte exercée par les hommes de fer*."[12] The abbé Fauchet, a member of the Cercle

Social and a future Girondin, wrote in the same vein that he would "die content, after having said only this: IT IS ARISTOCRACY WHICH CRUCIFIED THE SON OF GOD . . . Contemptible aristocrats deceived the masses which crawled before their pride; the masters induced into the empty souls of their slaves the rage that they themselves felt for the liberator of mankind." For Benoist Lamothe of Sens, Christ had been struck down by the fanaticism of the pharisees and "l'aristocratie judaïque."[13]

The social indeterminacy of *aristocratie* needs to be emphasized since it runs so counter to the historiographical implications of what Cobban called the "social Interpretation of the Revolution." Many texts could be cited to prove the fact that contemporaries took the socially amorphous nature of *aristocratie* for granted. As the *Journal républicain de Marseille* explained, "il y a des aristocrates dans toutes les classes; les uns par principes, par orgueil; les autres par intérêt, par préjugé, par routine moutonnière, et tous par méchanceté."[14] Because aristocracy was above all else an ethico-political principle, it could be found everywhere; "Parmi les aristocrates," wrote an imitator of the Père Duchesne, "il y a tant d'espèces différentes que cette bigarrure m'amuse bougrement. Il y en a qui sont de bonne foi, parce que leur intérêt personnel les frappe plus que l'intérêt général . . . . Ceux-là sont les moins à blâmer. D'autres le sont par fatuité, ou par entêtement. Ceux-là sont des jean-foutres méprisables."[15] Indeed, the plasticity of the term was so great that a chronicle of the Revolution could be organized around a list of the various social groups that were successively recognized by disconcerted Jacobins to have had heretofore unsuspected but now obvious aristocratic penchants. Historical hindsight sees this inimical blossoming as an effect of the Jacobins' growing social isolation. Convinced Revolutionaries perceived instead the malefic ability of *aristocratie* to find unexpected clients. In the words of the cautiously opportunistic Delisle de Salle, "il n'y a pas de formes que ne prennent les aristocrates pour se faire croire patriotes . . . [l'aristocratie] tout expirante qu'elle était, se reproduisait sans cesse sous de nouvelles formes."[16]

Importantly, however, even if the morally deceitful patriots of yesteryear or yesterday might suddenly prove to have been *aristocrates* all along, the physical manifestations of their treasonous condition, once it had been revealed, were unexpectedly constant. The French Revolution was a torrent, and in this

moving flood the political identity of the orthodox narrator was
forever changing: within a single year, from late 1791 to late
1792, revolutionary legitimacy was successively represented by
Barnave, Brissot, Danton, and Robespierre. But their varying
enemies, all of them *aristocrates*, however variegated they may
have been in the shape of their resistance to the Revolution (some
as monarchists, others as moderates, etc.), proved in retrospect to
have been curiously alike in their external and visible attributes.
Of necessity, no stable social or political portrait of the
aristocrate is to be found. But the physical and even moral
attributes of the socially protean aristocrat were constant because
aristocracy as a political option was forever embedded in the same
and darker side of human nature. Although aristocracy cannot be
defined in relationship to any set principle of politics, a telling
composite psychological and even physiological portrait of the
aristocrate can readily be assembled. Significantly, the materials
range here from the Feuillants' invectives against the *monarchiens*, to the Montagnards' accusations against both the Gironde
and the popular movement. Uniquely, high and low culture
converge in this matter since the rhetoric of condemnation is
remarkably of a kind, whether taken from newspapers, diaries,
plays, novels, eulogies, insults, broadsides, or accounts of private
conversations.

The aristocrat is everywhere described as selfish, secret,
insolent, and malicious (*méchant*). Above all, aristocrats are
"d'incurables égoïstes."[17] As the *Petit Catéchisme Français* laid
out, *aristocrates* are invariable concerned with their own "intérêt
particulier."[18] For the *Catéchisme des électeurs*, the various
aristocracies of birth, title, authority, abuse, wealth, the talents or
the professions are alike in that "toutes sont fondées sur un vil
intérêt."[19] "Ils n'eurent jamais d'autre roi, ni d'autre patrie, que
leur intérêt, leur orgueil, et leur vanité."[20] So was it therefore that
Marat thought on December 11, 1792, that the French Republic
had reached a turning point: it seemed impossible to him that
despotism and aristocracy could subsist because "l'égoïsme qui les
reproduit ne sauroit subsister."[21] Egoism and counter-revolution
went hand in hand: Was there "un seul canton dans la
république ou l'aristocratie de tous les genres, l'insouciance &
l'égoïsme ayent fait plus de ravages qu'à Lyon?"[22] Public
education was preferable to private schooling because the latter
was "propre à nourrir l'égoïsme et l'aristocratie."[23] Then too,
aristocrats were not only selfish, but corrupt also, and avaricious.

Sieyes in January 1789 prophetically laid out in his *Qu'est ce que le Tiers Etat?* the lines of the dichotomy: "pendant que les aristocrates parleront de leur honneur et veilleront à leur intérêt, le Tiers Etat, c'est-à-dire la nation, développera sa vertu, car si l'intérêt de Corps est l'égoïsme, l'intérêt national est vertu." Anarcharsis Cloots wrote of greed and pride that they were "les démons familiers de nos déraisonnables aristocrates."[24]

Since the aristocrat inverted the moral qualities of the patriot, aristocratic sociability was inevitably displayed as a parodic version of revolutionary camaraderie. The revolutionary *fête* unites the young and the aged, women and men, sans-culottes and jacobins, Parisians and provincials, Frenchmen and foreigners, the choir and the soloist, blacks and whites. Aristocratic sociability divides. Aristocracy is a perverse nation within the nation: it is a "peuplade,"[25] a "horde" which is "barbare dans ses vengeances."[26] Fantastically, for Anacharsis Cloots "*l'aristocratie* est fédéraliste, locale, isolée: la *sans-culotterie* n'est ni française, ni anglaise; elle est cosmopolite, universelle."[27] Concealment and hypocrisy likened the aristocrat to the witches of former times: like these demonic women, "la tourbe impure de l'aristocratie"[28] preferred to work in the "ténèbres." Aristocracy wears a mask. It was "dissimulée,"[29] and often concocted "un plan atroce et habilement combiné."[30]

Jacobinism inscribed itself in ahistorical nature and abstract reason. In perfect opposition to this elevation, aristocratism was a physicalized miasma that constantly evoked the vocabulary of medicine. Fauchet, not yet elected a Constitutional Bishop, in an address to the Cordeliers on November 21, 1789, referred to aristocracy as "une maladie si contagieuse qu'elle gagne presqu'inévitablement les meilleurs citoyens, dès le moment où ils ont obtenu les suffrages du peuple."[31] Aristocracy was often described as gangrenous,[32] a virus,[33] or kind of leprosy.[34] When Locquet de Grandville, a Breton nobleman soon to be executed, explained that his wife had died from grief at the death of her daughter, his judge inquired if this lady had not died of aristocracy instead?[35] Disease is also implied in the "rage rugissante de nos aristocrates."[36] Iconographically, the birth of aristocracy was presented as a purging of disease, as a kind of *lavement* or enema.[37]

Animalistic metaphors were also appropriate. The Père Duchesne wrote of his "grande joie de foutre la danse aux aristocrates qui osent lever la crête."[38] In July 1789, a group of

Parisian workers marched to the Champ de Mars behind a hearse decorated with toads, vipers, and rats, representing "la ruine du clergé et de l'aristocratie."[39] In April 1792, the patriots of Riez concluded that they would need dogs "pour donner la chasse aux aristocrates."[40] At Saint-Chamond, a Jacobin clubiste "déclame, gronde et tonne contre la gent aristocratique et fanatique . . . ajoutant que, si le sort de ces scélérats était à sa disposition, il le rendrait pire que celui des bêtes de somme et qu'il les exterminerait tous."[41] From the physicalization of aristocracy, the distance was short to its feminization as well: women, imagined by the Enlightenment to be particularly susceptible to disease and "vapors," were thought fated to *aristocratie*, which iconographically was often feminized. The reactionary hero of Mme de Staël's *Delphine* explained that "une femme ne saurait avoir trop d'aristocratie dans ses opinions."[42] The painter Jaurat, in what was described as a revolutionary canvas, represented aristocracy as a serpent, "caché sous les feuilles et dans l'intention de séduire [un] brave républicain; mais à l'instant ce monstre se voit pris au traquenard." In October 1793, the Montagnard Amar asked the Convention to abolish Women's Popular Societies on the grounds that aristocracy was using them to manipulate women, "pour les mettre aux prises avec les hommes."[43]

One saving advantage of this physicality in the age of Lavater was that a discerning Revolutionary physiognomist might recognize an aristocrat at a glance. Men and women were after all tolerably distinct; and in any case, aristocracy was readily identified elsewhere as well: aristocracy, wrote a journalist for the *Révolutions de Paris* on the occasion of the *fête* in honor of the mayor Simonneau who had been lynched during a food riot, "était peinte sur la physiognomie de la plupart des officiers qui ne portaient point la médaille en losange des gardes françaises."[44]

In actual practice, political opinions during the Revolution were at every point widely varied: the Feuillants had Jacobins to their left and *monarchiens* to their right. The Montagne located itself between Girondins and the sans-culottes. Hébert was to the left of Robespierre but to the right of the *enragés*. In the theorizing of the revolutionaries, however, the dichotomizing conceptualization of *aristocratie* and *patriotisme* repeatedly reduced these multiple distinctions to two. (The mechanism at work here bears obvious resemblence to other social/political dichotomies of bourgeois life, of men and women in the nineteenth century, of Aryans and Jews or whites and blacks in racist mythology.) It was in vain that Dupont de Nemours proclaimed himself in March 1791 to be "ni *Ministériel* ni *Aristocrate*, ni *Enragé*, mais bon Citoyen, ami de la Constitution . . . ."[45] Abroad, La Harpe, a Swiss, might write in 1791 to Catherine the Great that although "personne ne hait plus que moi la démocratie . . . je ne suis pas d'avantage *aristocrate*." Mme de Charrière, a Dutch woman living in Switzerland and a writer of great sensibility, likewise explained in July 1792 that she was "plus anti-aristocrate que je ne suis démocrate."[46] But inside France, subtle distinctions of this type could not hold. The *Grande Nation* was in the words of Robespierre "divisée en deux parties, le peuple et l'aristocratie."[47]

Understandably, conservative journalists tried to ridicule a term which ghettoized them politically and eventually threatened them with judicial pursuit. Mounier chuckled (briefly) over the thought that everyone in France including even little girls knew that "un aristocrate est un noble anthropophage qui se nourrit de la chair sanglante du peuple."[48]

Patriotic writers, needless to say, rose to that linguistic challenge: "J'ai lu, il y a bien longtemps," wrote Boissy d'Anglas in 1792, "& cela peut être pour la centième fois, que le mot *Aristocrate* étoit un mot vide de sens; et je n'ai pas compris comment cette observation avoit pu échapper à un homme accoutumé à réfléchir. Ce mot est sans doute une injure . . . mais il n'en est pas moins, une expression très-signifiante & très précise. Il désigne très clairement celui qui ne veut pas l'égalité . . . en un mot, un ennemi public."[49]

The debate had far-reaching effect because no other term in the political vocabulary of the times was more widely used: "Le terme est l'injure à la mode," Lescure observed in 1790, "les cochers de fiacre appellent aristocrates leurs chevaux rétifs, et les garçons traiteurs annoncent des 'aristocrates aux navets,' au lieu de 'dindons aux navets.'"[50] "Ce mot fatal," reflected Bertrand de Molleville, "devint dès ce moment [1789], le cri de ralliement contre tous ceux qui ne professoient pas le dévouement le plus aveugle . . . aux prétensions du tiers, qui exerçoit ainsi lui même l'aristocratie la plus tyrannique . . . ."[51]

Indeed, the term was so widely circulated and with such devastating result that it inclined contemporaries to reflect on the power of words, and on the strength also of the printed word: "Ce sont *les journalistes* qui, stipendiés pour échauffer les têtes et

tromper le peuple, ont eu le talent de lui rendre odieux sous le
nom d'aristocrates, qui signifie cependant dans son vrai sens, des
sages, d'excellens commandans: tous ceux qui l'ont fait travailler
ou vivre l'année dernière."[52] A journalist for La Quotidienne in
1797 expressed the same idea even more forecefully: "le mot
d'aristocrate a fait périr á lui seul plus de trois cents mille
français . . . . Notre révolution, bien analysée, est une révolution
de grammairiens qui se battent et qui s'égorgent pour détrôner
des mots, et notre liberté ressemble parfaitement à ces magiciens
de la féerie, qui bouleverseroient la nature en prononçant
quelques paroles baroques."[53]

2

In 1789-1792, the social content of the term had been gradually
subordinated to the political. But in 1793, aristocrate was once
more metamorphosed. Without losing its unnatural and even
animalistic connotations, the meaning of aristocrate shifted
towards the social once again, and it did so in an altogether new
way which suggestively prefigures the nineteenth century Marxist
vocabulary of social class.

The concept of an aristocracy of wealth was not of course
completely new in 1793. Already in 1784 Mably had urged
Americans to place obstacles in the way of "l'Aristocratie, and to
make laws to keep the rich from abusing their wealth and to buy
an authority which should not be theirs."[54] In 1789 and 1790
Charles de Lameth, Buzot, and Mme Roland also used the word
to describe a group that was economically defined. Marat was
working a well-known lode when he asked on June 30 1790:
"Qu'avons nous gagné à détruire l'aristocratie des nobles, si elle
doit être remplacée par l'aristocratie des riches?"[55]

The new idea of an aristocracy of wealth took solid root in
June 1790 during the debate on the abolition of the nobility; but
it was only in the summer of 1791 that Barnave clearly
conceptualized the new usage. After the king's flight to Varennes,
this most lucid of the Feuillant leaders recognized that the next
target of radicalized patriotism would necessarily be property
itself. In 1789, after the murder by the crowd of Bertier and
Foullon, Barnave, who was then courting allies on the left, had
asked rhetorically: "Ce sang était-il si pur?" But in late 1791,
Barnave now wished to resist the leftward drift of the Revolution
that had been precipitated by the king's flight. He urged the
propertied patriots of the National Assembly to find allies not on

the left, with Le Peuple, but on the right, with other owners of property who might or might not be dedicated patriots: "I ask from those who are listening to me here," he said, "if the nation is to experience more great shocks, if the Revolution is not to end now . . . I ask of you to answer this: is there another aristocracy remaining to be destroyed except for the aristocracy of property?"[56]

The same economic and political consciousness was reached from the other shore by the spokesmen and women of the popular movement (which of course must be carefully distinguished from bourgeois Jacobinism). By the spring of 1793, *enragés* like Leclerc d'Oze and Roux were also vocal in their belief that a new aristocracy of wealth had come into being. And on May 21, 1793, during a meeting of the Section of the Mail, in Paris, a sans-culotte pointed out that one could find "d'autres aristocrates. Ce sont tous les riches tous les gros marchands . . . ."[57] Two days later, in the Var, near Toulon, where Jacobinism had an Hébertist hue, local patriots similarly denounced "l'aristocratie des négociants épicuriens et cupides, qui frissonnent en entendant prononcer le seul mot d'Egalité."[58]

At first, however, the *enragés* used the new formulation incompletely. Leclerc for example did repeatedly take to task "une aristocratie bourgeoise et mercantile" whose paid agents deserved "la haine des patriotes."[59] But he did not push that idea very far. For him, the new mercantile aristocracy of 1793 was still part of a mixed group, that was "rusée, scélérate, malveillante, gangrenée, nobiliaire, sacerdotale," the tool of greed and of despots of all kinds. As the linguist Annie Geffroy, has observed, the *discours* of Leclerc is adjectivally oriented, and poor in concrete terms. Indeed, the most prominent and thoughtful leader of the *enragés*, Jacques Roux, was still thinking on June 25, 1793, of a multifaceted aristocracy, where the new mercantile aristocracy coexisted with "l'aristocratie nobilière et sacerdotale."[60] On July 17, 1793, he likewise denounced "les intrigues de l'aristocratie et du sacerdoce."

But on August 8, 1793, at the height of the *enragés'* power, Roux's vocabulary shifted one more time. It would be too strong to say that Roux now thought of aristocracy as a class in a Marxist sense that related politics to production, but he certainly did now perceive aristocracy as a single and articulated entity that rallied seemingly different groups around a single and all-important theme: money. Hence his attack on "l'aristocratie virulente des banquiers, des courtiers, des épiciers et des marchands de tous les états."[61]

Jacques Roux's linguistic shift is an important landmark in revolutionary usage, and may well express what is perhaps the most striking verbal change of the revolutionary decade taken as a whole. It is the analog on the left to Barnave's move of 1791 on the right. Before 1793, the revolutionary concept of *aristocratie* had made it possible for propertied and civic-minded Jacobins to link their more fundamental (and contradictory) desires: *nation*, *propriétés*, *libertés*, *fraternités*, and *justice*. Theirs was an unchallenged aporia of self-sacrifice and material self-enhancement. But Roux's new usage destroyed these linkages. Roux's linguistic turn exposed the now untenable ambiguities of a totalizing ethic that aimed to be universalist but which was, as Jaurès, Lefebvre, and so many others have quite rightly explained, nascently capitalist as well.

As is well known, the Montagnards' political response in November 1793 to the claims of the *enragés* and of the *hébertistes* was to reassert their control of the state, and to halt quite firmly the popular drive of dechristianization in both Paris and the provinces. What matters to our purpose here, however, is not high politics. Of greater relevance for us was the innovative effort of the Jacobins to locate aristocrats not just on the right, but at both extremes of the political debate as well, as citras and as ultras, as either *modérés* or *sectionnaires*.

Robespierre's use of the word *aristocrate* is revealing. Some months before, in the spring of 1793, when he had needed the sans-culottes to strike down the Gironde, the Incorruptible had at first inflected his use of the word *aristocrate* not *against* Roux, but *with* him. True, on April 10, 1793, before striking a tacit bargain with the plebs, Robespierre had still defined aristocracy politically and morally: "le système aristocratique . . . étoit celui de Lafayette et de tous ses pareils . . . il a été constitué par ceux qui ont succédé à sa puissance . . . le tout est semblable; les moyens sont les mêmes . . . ."[62] But on May 8, 1793, (only three weeks before the expulsion of the Girondins through the joint efforts of the Mountain and the sans-culottes whom he courted actively, Robespierre had begun to look at the issue in a different and more social way: the spirit of aristocracy, he wrote, "n'est réclamée aujord'hui ni par les prêtres ni les ci-devants nobles, mais par la classe des marchands . . . ."[63] Indeed, Robespierre persisted in this second and populist mode for some time: on

February 2, 1794, he might still write in a private note: "Je crois qu'il faut tuer l'aristocratie mercantile comme on a tué celle des prêtres et des nobles."

On February 5, 1794, however, in a vast and public programmatic statement, Robespierre now felt once again that the time had come for him to return to his antecedent definition of aristocracy, which had of course been much less social and much more political than Roux's. The essence of *aristocratie*, he decided after having broken the dechristianizers' campaign, was not economic individualism at all, as the *enragés* had come to assume, but an insubordinate will to power, especially by those whose task it was to obey the Jacobins: "la démocratie périt par deux excès, l'aristocratie de ceux qui gouvernent ou le mépris du peuple pour les autorités." "L'aristocratie se constitue en sociétés."[64] Some weeks later on April 16, 1794, Roberspierre went one step further—or back: the sans-culottes' banquets set up in the streets of Paris after the banning of the sans-culottes' section meetings only *appeared* to be fraternal. These covertly anti-jacobin feasts, he now realized, had in fact been inspired by the aristocracy. Aristocrats, it seemed, even knew how to turn republican virtue against the Republicans themselves: "un des secrets les plus dangereux de l'aristocratie, est de faire dans un temps ce qui n'est bon à faire que dans un autre . . . . Il ne faut pas que l'aristocratie puisse accuser la Convention de ne pas aimer la fraternité."[65]

Predictably, the last gasp of Jacobin linguistic universalism before thermidor was to use the accusation of aristocracy against the poor: "Faites respecter l'autorité légitime," opined the Montagnard administrators of the Department of the Hautes Pyrénées, "et l'insolente aristocratie déguisée sous le masque du patriotisme, se verra anéantie."[66] On January 27, 1794, Jeanbon Saint-André in the Jacobin club had at Paris also reminded his listeners that they should not trust the leaders of the popular left, "arrivé(s) soudain dans la Révolution, exagérant le patriotisme . . . ."

3

During the years of the Directory, communist usage followed the patterns set by the *enragés* in the summer of 1793, while the Thermidorians followed the examples of the Robespierrists in the early spring of 1794, yet another reminder that the turning point and decline of Jacobinism does not come in thermidor of the year

II, but in the late winter of 1793-1794 with the growing separation of the popular from the propertied.

Not surprisingly, the extreme left in 1794-1799 (whether popular or Babouvian) routinely followed *enragé* precedent and used the word *aristocrate* to describe not just anti-republicans but the propertied Jacobins as well. For the populist habitués of the Café des Cannoniers, in January, "Jacobin ou aristocrate est synonyme."[67] Similarly, Babeuf on November 7, 1794 denounced "une aristocratie mille fois plus tyrannique que celle de la noblesse et du clergé . . . l'aristocratie des agioteurs et des fripons."[68] For him, the Thermidorians were only "d'infâmes valets de l'aristocratie constitutionnelle."

For the non-thermidorian Crest, that is to say for the left Montagnards in the Convention, many of whom like Romme and Soubrany (a genuine marquess, as it happens) soon became the "martyrs de prairial," aristocracy was in some respects as the Babouvians defined it, and in others not. For these left, propertied but still universalist-minded Jacobins who felt nostalgia for the Jacobin/sans-culottes alliance of the spring of 1793, only *some* forms of wealth were *aristocrates*. Goujon for example explained on August 22, 1794 that Alsace was riddled with the "agents contre-révolutionnaires de la Suisse" and by the "aristocratie des riches," but he quickly added that the supporters of these wealthy aristocrats were not typical owners of property: Goujon's contempt was reserved for priests and for a "foule de juifs, tous agioteurs . . . ." In a speech of September 17, 1794, largely devoted to the question of aristocracy, Collot d'Herbois, a Jacobin populist, also tried to steer a middle course between an economic and a moralizing stance: all over France, he explained, patriots were being oppressed by a reviving aristocracy. However, he did not define this group as coterminous with the possessing class generally. Collot's *aristocrates* were only the stock-jobbing, nouveaux-riches, corrupt and orgiastic owners of new property. The aristocrats whom Jacobins might fear were only those men who wanted a compromise peace, "qui voudraient dissoudre la Convention . . . ceux qui se sont attachés à toutes les factions . . . ces hommes pour qui le crime est un besoin . . . [and who were to be found] dans les lieux les plus méprisables . . . dans les boudoirs impurs des courtisanes . . . au milieu des orgies les plus dégoûtantes."[69]

Needless to say, the ideologically "progressive," republican, but socially conservative Thermidorians violently disagreed with both the popular left and the Crest on this score. For these chastened Jacobins, who wanted the poor to believe that social forms were transparent, the correct definition of aristocracy was to be found in the last and "non-social" usage of Robespierre, though they did not of course dwell on that filiation. Aristocrats there certainly were, thought these friends of Sieyes, but aristocrats were on the extreme left and right of their own Republican and Directorial orthodoxy. On October 3, 1794, the mainstream Conventionnel Laporte denounced the "caste d'hommes privilégiés qui se prétendent les patriotes exclusifs et traitent d'aristocrates tous ceux qui n'ont pas obtenu d'eux des certificats de civisme dans leurs orgies. (Applaudissements.)"[70] Indignantly, on June 1, 1796, the pro-government newspaper the *Anti-Terroriste* attacked the "patriotes exclusifs" who dared to present the regime's supporters as the "aristocratie des riches."[71] It was fortunate, concluded the sheet, that the "croassements (des) apôtres du brigandage se perdent dans le vague des airs." In August 1796, Mailhe, once a Montagnard but now a Thermidorian, took on the Babouvists "qui traitent cette constitution d'aristocratique parce que les intrigants et les voleurs ne pourront y trouver leur compte." Mercier too in 1798 mocked "Babeuf et . . . sa clique" qui "appelant aristocrates et suspects tout ceux qui avaient une bibliothèque ou une pendule, s'apprêtoit à mettre sous les scellés tous les meubles de notre succession, comme devant être légalement partagés."[72] Aristocrats were just as Robespierre had said they were, on the far left and on the right, as either citras or ultras. The department of the Var, explained a governmental agent, had been taken over by "anarchistes" and that of the Bouches-du-Rhône, by "aristocrates."[73] From the regime's point of view, the two extremes were really of one kind, and perhaps even in basic accord: "les bourreaux de l'aristocratie étoient les mêmes qui s'étoient déjà vendus aux Robespierristes. L'aristocratie n'a fondé ses fureurs décuplés que sur cette populace, le fléau de tous les gouvernements, et l'instrument féroce de tous les partis."[74] A representative of the central Thermidorian government explained in a report that the left-wing troublemakers of his district were "semblables en tout aux anciens aristocrates."[75] It is from a similar point of view, finally, that the governmental newspaper, *L'ami des lois*, reasoned that "si les terroristes se sont déclarés les ennemis des aristocrates, c'était uniquement pour complaire à Louis XVIII."[76]

The thermidorian use of the term coincided perfectly with the fundamental goal of the regime, which was to mobilize a hypothetically Republican possessing class on two fronts: as

ideological progressives against the right, and as social conservatives against the far left. La Revellière-Lépeaux, some few days
after the coup of fructidor against the parliamentary right in
September 1797, described what that "touchant accord" of
propertied Republicans might achieve: "puissent tous les
républicains se rallier, et des nuances d'opinion ne plus les rendre
le jouet de l'aristocratie et du fanatisme. Puisse le terrorisme que
les uns affectent de craindre, et que les autres voudroient en effet
rendre redoutable, pour nous faire jeter dans les bras du
royalisme, ne plus servir de prétexte pour arrêter les progrès de
l'esprit public."[77]

Gradually, the word itself became risible. From 1789 to 1794, as
has been said, no other political term had been more frequently
used, and more expressive of the spirit of the Revolution.
Gibbon, conservative and worried, wrote in May 1792 that
"Lanterns hang in every street . . . *Aristocrate* in every mouth."
By 1795, however, a shrewd observer noted already that "the word
aristocrate which has cost their lives for thousands of citizens, is
beginning to wear out."[78] And in 1796, a traveller, when asked by
the secretary of the Section of the Arsenal to identify himself as
an aristocrat or a moderate, thought fit to reply that he was
neither: "No, Sir. I am a knife-grinder."[79]

4

One of the most striking particularities of the French
Revolution was its insertion of a potentially capitalistic *discours*
into a semantically elaborate and quasi-religious rhetoric of
universalist equality. For the Jacobins, who were, as it happens,
avid purchasers of *biens-nationaux*, social categories were not of
interest. Society was in a sense to be defiantly ignored. Given the
course of European society in the next century, the intense
paradox of the French Revolution was to set its defense of private
individualism (of which institutionalized capitalism soon became
the first effect) within a culturally and politically demanding
system of public life that asserted the universalist claims of
republican *civisme*. For the Jacobins of either the left (the
Montagnards) or the right (the Girondins), individual self-
assertions were also communitarian statements. From 1789 to
1793, the first and persistent goal of revolutionaries of all hues
from Barnave to Marat was—and in much the same terms—to
conciliate the rights of individuated and propertied, Enlightened
man (women were decidely excluded by both Jacobins and

hébertistes) to the responsibilities of citizenship as it had
supposedly been defined in Greco-Roman times. They aimed to
fuse the rights of what would soon become capitalist property to
an adamant cult of civic sacrifice. In 1793, that vision began to
falter. In 1795-1799, it collapsed.

1789 was the Revolution of fraternity, half-way between the
liberty of 1776 and the "demo-socs" of 1848. Chamfort may not
have been wrong to think that in practice, Revolutionary
fraternity often meant "sois mon frère, ou je te tue." An accepted
"aristocrate converti" (from the title of a play by Couthon of
1791) was a *rara avis*. At the same time, of course, the French
Revolution did politicize our culture's fraternal aspirations as no
other doctrine had before and as no other has since dared to try.
Has any political statement ever elicited the enthusiastic
unanimity of the Fête de la Fédération on the first anniversary of
July 14, 1789? In that sense if in no other, the Revolution must
be seen as a genuinely progressive moment in world history, a
moment whose meaning transcends both the collapse of the
monarchy and the substitution of merit and wealth to birth and
caste as the organizing principles of western culture.

Of this revolutionary sense of fraternity, as we have tried to
show, "aristocracy" was the perfect antithesis as appears perhaps
from the most acute definition of the term given in 1828 by
Babeuf's admirer, Buonarroti: *aristocratie*: "pouvoir souverain
exercé par une partie de la nation sur le tout . . . suite inévitable
de l'inégalité consacrée par l'ordre égoïste."[80]

NOTES

I am grateful to Margaret Higonnet and Sandy Petrey for their help and advice
on the structure and form of this essay.

1. Cited by Murray Forsythe, *Reason and Revolution: The Political Thought
of the Abbé Sieyes* (New York, 1987), 63, 77, and 107.

2. In this introduction to Fichte's *Considérations sur la Révolution Française*
(Paris, 1974), 24.

3. J.J. Rousseau, *The Social Contract*, trans. Ernest Barker (Oxford, 1977),
Book 3, parts 4 and 5.

4. *De la Vérité* (Paris, 1782), 165-166, quoted in G.A. Kelly, *Victims,
Authority, and Terror* (Chapel Hill, 1982).

5. Quoted in Decouflé, *L'Aristocratie française devant l'opinion publique*, 31.

6. Montignot, *Réflexions sur les immunités écclésiastiques considérées dans
leur rapport avec les maximes du droit public et de l'intérêt national* (Paris, 1788),
138. Lescure in 1791 still distinguished between court nobles and "la partie de la
noblesse qui (avant 1789) était la plus maltraitée par l'aristocratie de faveur [qui]

forme un parti à part, et réclame les principes mêmes de la nouvelle Constitution pour l'égalité."

7. See George Kelly, *Victims, Authority, and Terror*, 45.
8. *Discours*, ed. François Furet (Paris, 1973), 60.
9. *Journal Politique National*, ed. De Spens (Paris, 1964), 100.
10. June 14, 1791, Ferrières, *Correspondance* (Paris, 1932), 370.
11. June 7, 1791, *L'Ami du Peuple*, no. 460, 5.
12. See *Le procès de Socrates, ou le régime des anciens temps*. This play was performed in Paris on November 9, 1790.
13. Claude Fauchet, *Discours sur la liberté française*, 8, and Frank Bowman, *Le Christ Romantique* (Geneva, 1973), 77.
14. *Journal républicain de Marseille*, October 13, 1793, no. 6, 44.
15. *Le Père Duchesne*, 29th letter, 6; for the authenticity of this letter, see F. Braesch, *Le Père Duchesne d'Hébert* (Paris, 1938), 77, note 6.
16. Cited by Pierre Malandain, *Delisle de Sales, philosophe de la nature, 1714-1816* (Oxford, 1984), 384. During the fêtes de la Réunion of August 1793, the Quotidienne similarly observed that "l'aristocratie a pris cent formes diverses, ie peuple tout puissant l'a partout terrassée" (2).
17. According to Collot d'Herbois, April 1, 1793, Aulard ed., *Recueil*, 3:301.
18. *Le Petit Catéchisme Français* (F.S.), 3:37.4.
19. In 1791/1792. F.S. 3:39.6. Bibliothèque Historique de Paris.
20. According to Mercier, *Le Nouveau Paris*, 1:31.
21. *Journal de la République française*, no. 3, 17 and 4.
22. Marat, March 21, 1793, *Le Publiciste*, no. 49, 4.
23. *Le Démocrate*, October 30, 1794, no. 5, 3.
24. *Opinion d'Anacharsis Cloots, Instruction Publique, Spectacles* (Paris an II).
25. February 7, 1798, *L'Anti-royaliste ou le Républicain du Midi*, 21:82.
26. *Révolution de Paris*, No. 64. (September 2, 1790), 593.
27. *Opinion d'Anacharsis Cloots, Instruction Publique, Spectacles* (Paris an II), 8, note 1.
28. Aulard, *La Société des Jacobins*, on December 26, 1793, 579.
29. The abbé Fauchet, *Second discours sur les libertés françaises* (Paris, 1789), 2.
30. De Lescuree, 2:392. October 15, 1789.
31. Lacrois, *Les Assemblées des représentants de la Commune de Paris*, première série, 3:22.
32. Leber, *L'Assemblée des noirs*, 4:19.1.
33. Lescure, September 1790, *Journal*, 2:474.
34. *Projet de Discours sur les causes des malheurs de la République Française*, *Scripta Roux*, ed. Markov, 126.
35. Olivier Blanc, *La Dernière lettre* (Paris, 1983), 134.
36. De Lescure, *Journal*, February 26, 1791, 2:508.
37. See for example the *Naissance des Aristocrates. Le Lavement a produit son effet, au Diable le fumet*, Collection Hennin, no. 10594, 120:68.
38. *Le Père Duchesne*, no. 243.
39. Cited in Mona Ozouf, *La Fête révolutionnaire* (Paris, 1976), 58.
40. Cited in Jacques Guilhaumou, "Le Commissaire Isoard," in *Mouvements populaires* (Paris, 1985), 547.
41. Cited by Colin Lucas, *The Structure of the Terror: the Example of Javoques and the Loire* (Oxford, 1973), 115.
42. *Delphine* (Paris, 1981), 469.

43. The 9th brumaire, year II, in the Convention, *Le Moniteur*, 18:300.

44. In June 1792, cited in Mona Ozouf, *La Fête révolutionnaire*, 85.

45. *Supplément au journal de Paris*, no. 65, March 6, 1791.

46. *Oeuvres Complètes*, 3:393. Mme de Charière cherished these ambiguities. In her unpublished comedy of 1794 entitled *Les vous et les tois*, Bertrands accuses Francoeur of being "Aristocratiquement Démocrate" (*Oeuvres* [Genève, 1977], 7:377).

47. In the National Assembly on February 22, *Oeuvres complètes*, 6:239-40.

48. In 1790, cited by Gallais, *Extrait d'un dictionnaire inutile*. "Aristocrate, c'est le *haro* qui ordonne, qui oblige, qui force tout bon français à courir sus, à s'emparer de l'individu quelconque taxé ou prévenu d'aristocratie" in *Dictionnaire national et anecdotique* 1790, cited by Guilhaumou, *Dictionnaire des usages socio-politiques*.

49. Boissy d'Anglas, *Quelques Idées sur la Liberté, la Révolution, le Gouvernement républicain, et la Constitution Française*, June 5, 1792, 15. Loustalot in his *Révolutions de Paris* of November 7-14, 1789 made the same point: "on a tenté a nous persuader que ce mot (d'aristocrate) est devenu insignifiant . . . nous n'avons pas donné dans le piége." And again, 30 juillet-6 août 1791, "Citoyens! . . . on vous tend un piège . . . Il consiste à substituer au mot "vielli" d'aristocrates celui de modérés, et à la qualification de patriotes celles de factieux." (Cited by Guilhaumou, *Dictionnaire des usages socio-politique du français sous la Révolution*).

50. De Lescure, *Journal*, on January 2, 1790, 2:413. Lescure recounts another anecdote in this same genre: "l'abbé Maury pressoit . . . le cocher d'un fiacre qui le conduisoit. Celui-ci fouette ses chevaux en criant: "B . . . d'aristocrate!" —Est-ce que tu me connois?" dit l'abbé. "Non, mon bourgeois."—"Qui appelles tu donc aristocrate?"—"C'est la bête que j'ai sous la main: elle ne tire pas, elle laisse faire toute la besogne à l'autre" (2:428). Chatreau in his *Dictionnaire national et annecdotique* of 1790 also comments that "le "mot d'aristocrate est devenu une injure que les gens du peuple se prodiguent entre eux. Les forts de la halle, en entrant au cabaret, demandent un demi-setier de vin aristocrate; cela veut dire du vin à 15s."

51. Bertrand de Molleville.

52. *Enfin, Qui est-ce donc qui a gagné la révolution?* Bibliothèque Nationale, 1790, Lb 39 3160A, 14.

53. *La Quotidienne*, on April 19, 1797, no. 359, 1-2.

54. Mably, *Observations sur le Gouvernment et les loix des Etats-Unis d'Amérique* (Amsterdam, 1784), 25.

55. Marat, June 30, 1790, *Supplique de dix-huit millions d'infortunés privés de leurs droits de citoyens actifs*, cited by Ragon, *Histoire de la littérature prolétarienne en France*, 71.

56. J.J. Chevalier, *Barnave* (Paris, 1936), 283.

57. Procès verbal de la section du Mail, *Die Sansculotten von Paris, Dokumente zur Geschichte der Volksbewegung*, ed. Markov and Soboul (East Berlin, 1793-1794), doc. 8, 48.

58. At Saint-Zacharie, cited by Henri Labroue, *Le Club Jacobin de Toulon (1790-1796)* (Paris, 1907), 35.

59. We are following here Annie Geffroy's excellent essay, "Trois successeurs de Marat pendant l'été de 1793, analyse lexicométrique des spécificités" *Mots* (October 1980).

60. Cited by Guérin, *La Lutte des classes sous la première république* (Paris, 1946), i.78.

61. August 8, 1793, *Le publiciste*, no. 254, *Scripta Roux*, ed. Markov, 220.

62. *Oeuvres*, 9 (Paris, 1958): 377.

63. *Oeuvres*, 9:486.

64. 17 pluviôse an II, *Archives Parlementaires* (Paris, 1962), 335.

65. *Oeuvres*, 10:534.

66. July 2, 1794, *Archives Parlementaires* (Paris, 1980), 92:336.

67. Police report, *Paris sous la réaction thermidorienne*, Aulard ed., 1:364.

68. Babeuf, in November 1795, *Le Tribun du Peuple*, no. 35, 100.

69. September 11, 1794, *Le Moniteur* (Paris, 1847), 21:733-34.

70. October 5, 1794, *Le Moniteur* (Paris, 1842), 22:137.

71. June 1, 1796, *L'Anti-Terroriste*, no. 12, 146.

72. Mercier, *Nouveau Paris* (1798-99), 6:29.

73. Despinassy, July 7, *Recueil*, Aulard ed., 25:236. It is worth noting that the tripartite distinction *anarchiste/patriote/aristocrate* was used locally well before thermidor in the southeast, where mainstream jacobins often were confronted not only by royalists but also by an "hébertiste" or populist alliance of popular revolutionaries and left-leaning jacobins, often of artisanal rather than of bourgeois origin.

74. Louis Sébastien Mercier, *Le Nouveau Paris* (Paris, 1798), 1:xxi.

75. December 28, 1794, *Recueil*, Aulard ed., 19:145.

76. August 19, 1799, *Le Démocrate ou le défenseur des principes*, no. 17, 3.

77. *Le Démocrate, Journal politique et littéraire*, September 14, 1797, no. 5, 2.

78. *Essai sur le patriotisme* (s.l.n.d) Bibliothèque Nationale, Lb41 4529, 1.

79. In a police report dated January 28, 1796, *Paris pendant la réaction thermidorienne*, 2:716. This remark might relate to a type of political joke. The same pleasantry appears in a play of Mme de Charrière entitled *Elise ou l'Université*, in *Oeuvres* (Genève, 1979), 7:418: "Eugénie: Un moment Caroline. Etes vous Démocrate ou aristocrate? Caroline: Je suis femme de chambre."

80. Buonarotti, *Conspiration pour l'égalité dite de Babeuf* (Paris, 1957), 1:32, note 1.

HEROISM IN THE FEMININE: THE EXAMPLES OF CHARLOTTE CORDAY AND MADAME ROLAND

Chantal Thomas

In *Les Femmes de la Révolution*, Jules Michelet examines the revolutionary role of women and pronounces a judgement that, initially enthusiastic, slides progressively toward overt condemnation. He first considers women dynamic and decisive elements because their constant contact with daily needs, their family responsibilities, and the torments caused by disease and hunger made them suffer the most from the harshness of the Ancien Régime. They had a physical, vital impetus to struggle for its abolition. It was as *privileged victims* that they became the most determined insurgents. Michelet's vision applies to the women of the people taken as a group, fantasized as beings of pure generosity and unforeseen impulses. Their energy triumphed on October 6, 1789, when they forced the royal family to leave Versailles for Paris. "Men made July 14, women October 6."[1] Michelet continued: "The first expedition, dominated by women, quite spontaneous, quite naive, was, one might say, determined by needs, and it shed no blood."[2] But it is this same spontaneity, or this excessive sensibility, that makes women credulous and undependable, subject to the profound influence of priests and religion,[3] finally more often agents fatal to the Revolution than artisans of its success.

Michelet concludes: "If women first added a new flame to revolutionary enthusiasm, it must also be said that, driven by a blind sensibility, they soon contributed to the reaction and, even when their influence was most respectable, often prepared the death of political parties."[4] Once the equivalence of woman and sensibility (if not instinct) is asserted, it is logical to conclude on the incompatibility of woman and Revolution, for the latter understood itself as the triumph of Reason. This incompatibility is in a funny and pathetic way apparent in a portrait of Mademoiselle Maillard, singer, hanging in the Musée Carnavalet. Who is this young lady? Why has her name been preserved for posterity? Because of her voice? No, because of an extraordinary performance, for which her singing was unquestionably not a qualification. A note informs us that "she embodied the goddess Reason during the atheist ceremony of November, 1793, in the desacralized cathedral of Notre Dame." The goddess has a round, quite fleshy face and small brown eyes. Her curly hair is adorned with a red ribbon matching the imperial mantle laid across her shoulders. Her breasts are broadly exposed. She says with all her facile sensuousness that this is a perverse miscasting or, more seriously, that Reason is not to be incarnated, that it lacks a taste for pleasure.

As reserves of insurrectional energy, women (those "good old she-devils" Père Duchesne approvingly mentioned when discussing the market women of the Halles and the shopkeepers of the Palais Royal) were not to individualize themselves into singular figures. Their other recognized function, one connected not to stormy violence but to representation, consisted of participation in the festivals of the Revolution. It was a decorative function and made women into anonymous props: the beauty of Mademoiselle Maillard was supposed to be absorbed by the triumph of Reason. In their festive role as in their taste for insurgency, they were valued above all for their group effect, for their power of numbers. In July, 1791, the *Gazette universelle* reported the parade of the "Amies de la Constitution de Bordeaux" that brought together three or four thousand women (July 7). The same paper gave the details of another huge female ceremony that took place in Tours (July 17): "It was decided that the female group would march in two lines, the right line being composed of mothers; that the uniform headpiece would be white gauze with an attached cockade of the national colors; that hair would be tightly bound into a bun; that the uniform would be a white jacket with matching skirt, slit up the side, each part laced to the other by a light green ribbon revealing a pink garment beneath. It was also decided that a tricolor ribbon worn as a sash would replace belts."[5] Such initiatives met with great approbation. They came from women's clubs that, as Paule-Marie Duhet writes, "even in the summer of 1791 still . . . seemed vacuous and decorative."[6]

The acceptable option for women was thus either to stir up anger for uprisings or to become images of wisdom. They could choose between two allegories: one was violent and showed justice claiming its rights; the other was peaceful and showed radiant motherhood and republican virtue. At a time when the political scene was for the first time in the history of France showing public confrontations between party leaders powerfully endowed with eloquence, options and personality, at a time when intelligence and talent found full scope in legislative proposals, government programs, newspaper articles, wall posters, assembly speeches, and on and on, women were reduced to silence (their screams were admissible when they blended into a crowd's) or consecrated to the sacrificial effacement of wife and mother. The contrast is shocking. It was bitterly resented by numerous women who wanted effective participation and needed something more than the right to be either an incitement or a figuration.

Only Condorcet, in his *Essai sur l'admission des femmes au droit de cité* (1790), proposed responding affirmatively to women's demands. His text produced no concrete measures. Women were officially excluded from political rights by the constitution of 1793. There was consequently something of the outlaw, something transgressive in the few women who, in this male-permeated atmosphere, succeeded in making themselves illustrious. They could do so only by desiring the Revolution in spite of the very norms it imposed on them as women, only by adhering to virile models. The women of 1789 were set before a classic double bind: remain women, but deny themselves all exaltation and all heroic action, or else attain the sublime, but transgress the ideal reserved for their sex. The latter was the course spectacularly chosen by Charlotte Corday and followed more diplomatically (she was a politician and not a terrorist) by Madame Roland.

1

The one who, from the point of view of celebrity and effectiveness of her deed, produced the most masterful stroke (in all senses of the word) was obviously Charlotte Corday, whose daring and tranquillity in murder continue to fascinate. Charlotte Corday belonged to a noble and poor family of Normandy. Having lost her mother at a very early age, she read a great deal and was just as enthusiastic about her religious education in a convent as about the thought of Rousseau she discovered in secret. The Rousseauist fervor in which she grew up allowed the young woman to make this assertion during her interrogation: "I was a republican long before the Revolution." She was living in Caen when the Revolution began, the city where in June of 1793 the Girondist deputies who had been expelled from the Assembly came to seek refuge. That was how she crossed paths with

Barbaroux, Pétion and Louvet, enemies of Marat. What she heard from them confirmed her in her resolution, but she owed her decision to herself alone. Charlotte Corday had neither accomplice nor confidante. The force with which her act is inscribed and its impact on the imagination are inextricable from her solitude and the lightning rapidity of her conception and execution.

Charlotte Corday wished for a Republic like the Utopia of ancient Greece or republican Rome. She placed it under the sign of peace and harmony. In one of her last letters, Madame Roland confided in the same spirit, "It is true that I wanted freedom only with justice, wisdom only in pleasing forms."[7] For Charlotte Corday the problem was simple. Through an association, typical of the revolutionary mentality, that confused political error with the forces of evil, there was but one obstacle to the coming of "good form": Marat. Therefore his elimination was all that was needed for France to reach the new era of happiness and freedom. Charlotte Corday was led to perform her murderous act as peremptorily as Joan of Arc was led to restore the sovereignty of her King. The two of them had the same motive: the salvation of France. But Charlotte Corday, unlike Joan of Arc, did not receive her call from a divine message. It came only from her reading. "Her head," a journalist wrote during her trial, "was a fury of readings of every sort."[8]

In reality, her basic inspiration was the lives narrated by Plutarch, the only book she took on her one-way trip to Paris. Charlotte Corday's predilection for Plutarch clearly shows her detachment from daily life. Manifestly, she did not assess her life on the horizon of the probable. Her ambition was as lofty as that displayed by Pyrrhus, Alexander, Brutus, Otho, Alcibiades. It was beside their destinies as men of war and political leaders, beside their bloody exploits and violent deaths that she wanted to measure herself. Her existence would make sense only in *parallel* with the courage of those supermen.

Such fever for heroism, fed by Plutarch, is doubly literary, for it also echoes a childhood memory found in Rousseau's *Confessions*: "Plutarch became my favorite author. The pleasure I took in endlessly reading him cured me somewhat of novels; and I soon preferred Agesilaus, Brutus and Aristides to Orondate, Artamène and Juba. From those interesting readings, from the conversations they opened between my father and me, was formed this free and republican spirit, this indomitable and proud character, impatient with yoke and servitude, that has all my life tormented me in the situations least suited to its expression. Ceaselessly concerned with Athens and Rome, living so to speak with their great men, myself born the citizen of a republic, the son of a man whose greatest passion was love of the fatherland, I caught fire from his example, I believed myself a Greek or a Roman."[9] For Rousseau, the image of the father was superimposed on dead heroes, in the same way that the Republic of Geneva continued Athens and Rome. His readings, hallucinatory though they are, were anchored in the present. Charlotte Corday, on the other hand, lived the tragic Stoicism of Plutarch's characters against a background of religiosity and in a mystical intimacy that made no distinction between heroism and holiness. When confused with love of God, love of the fatherland precludes any adjustment to reality. In the same way, it cannot be satisfied by imaginary identifications. The Christian woman is enjoined to follow the example of the Virgin Mary, not to think she is the Virgin. Madame Roland, like Charlotte Corday, read Plutarch with the impression that she was receiving the Truth. For her as well, this revelation was deeply religious in tone. The *Memoirs* she wrote in prison are explicit. "But Plutarch seemed to be the real nourishment suited to me; I will never forget Lent of 1763 (I was then nine years old), when I took his book to Church and pretended it was a missel. That was the beginning of the impressions and ideas that made me a republican without my even dreaming of becoming one."[10]

All his life Rousseau sought tests through which to prove the strength of his soul; and, in a way, his paranoia was a reaction to the failure of suffering inscribed in the reality of his epoch. Thanks to the Revolution, Charlotte Corday and Madame Roland could fully live the tone of republican fervor set by the religious feelings of their childhoods. They had the "luck" to find objective situations. The specificity of Charlotte Corday is that, like an artist, she wanted to create her great moment by herself and give it the greatest possible theatricality. That is why her first plan was to assassinate Marat on July 14, 1793, in the Champ de Mars. Then she chose the National Assembly. She wanted a public space, a site where the execution would have a great number of spectators. She resolved to go to Marat's house (she just couldn't accept the domestic stage of bourgeois theater) only after learning that Marat's sickness prevented him from attending the Assembly's sessions. After being refused admission on her first visit, she wrote a letter: "my great unhappiness is enough for me to have a right to your good will." This was the only duplicity in her actions, and she excused herself for it at her trial. The visitor was about to be prevented from entering for a second time, but Marat, at the sound of her voice ("her almost childlike voice" according to the testimony of her lawyer) intervened.

Charlotte Corday was tried and condemned on July 17 and executed the same day, dressed in the red mantle of the parricide. Her serene calm all along the route to the guillotine did not belie the sentence she wrote before her execution: "I have for two days enjoyed a delightful peace."

Charlotte Corday's act immediately had great repercussions. Independently of the victim, the deed of a young girl assassinating a man in his bathtub was bound to strike a powerful chord. As a woman, Charlotte Corday at first aroused insatiable fury on the part of revolutionary women, who were both distressed because of their attachment to Marat and anxious not to be objects of the antifeminism Charlotte Corday's murder was bound to provoke. Charlotte Corday said that, when she was arrested at the scene of the crime, what most distressed her was the violence of the women present: " . . . as I was truly calm, I suffered from the shouts of a few women. But to save your country means not noticing what it costs."[11] Among these women's shouts were surely those of Marat's widow, who soon afterwards made this public declaration: she "denounces to the universe" the crime of Charlotte Corday. "The memory of Marat is the only property left to her, she wishes to consecrate to its defense the final days of a languishing life."[12]

More vigorous was the address of the Society of Revolutionary Republican Women, who declared "that they will people the land of liberty with as many Marats as children borne by the Revolutionary Republican Women, that they will raise these children in the cult of Marat, and swear to put in their hands no gospel other than Marat's works, with verses in his memory, and curse the infernal fury brought forth by the race of Caen."[13] To eliminate all appearance of solidarity with a woman's fanatical act against the Friend of the People was all the more necessary for Jacobin women because they were living in a political context where Queen Marie-Antoinette represented the scourge of the Ancien Régime, where pamphlet, press and word of mouth circulated the idea that every vice to be stamped out was to be stigmatized in the person of a woman. At the limit, in an echo of the Biblical myth of Eve's original sin, republican France had to be regenerated from a state of corruption engendered and perpetuated by a harpy who was the wife of Louis XVI "le bon."

Among men, Charlotte Corday's knife thrust, so well placed that her prosecutor asked if she had practiced ("Oh, the monster!" cried the indignant Charlotte Corday. "He takes me for an assassin!"[14]) produced a panic effect, particularly among the deputies of the Montagne who, interpreting the young woman's deed as the fruit of a Girondist plot, saw themselves constantly threatened by lurking killers. During her trial, there was a concerted but vain effort to make Charlotte Corday confess the names of her accomplices and instigators, an attempt to treat her as the mere instrument of a project fomented by others. Public opinion designated her through terms like "faction of scoundrels" or "enemies of the people." Jean-Pierre Marat and Marie Brousson, brother and sister of Jean-Paul Marat, in their deposition calling for "exemplary punishment of the traitor," avoided using the name Charlotte Corday. They went so far as to write that "their brother was assassinated by a scoundrel wearing woman's clothes."[15]

Charlotte Corday was conscious that the meaning of the refusal opposed to her act went beyond the political conflicts opposing Montagnards and Girondists. She understood the vehemence quite well. "No one is satisfied," she wrote, "to have a mere woman without consequence to offer to the spirit of that great man."[16] In reality, and she knew it, it was not without consequence that she was a woman. The will to dispossess her of her act was applied precisely to that "monstrous," "denatured" femininity that dared measure itself against the greatness even of Marat and that beat him on his home court. David expressed with particular clarity the refusal of Charlotte Corday, the scandal of her existence. All he had to do was erase Charlotte Corday from the pictoral representation of Marat's death. As Gilbert Lascault has argued, "A criminal femininity endangered his desire for a revolutionary sacerdocy and his apology of Marat. From the painted field he excluded Charlotte Corday."[17]

The violence of David's censorship of Charlotte Corday was perpetuated in the way Gérard Walter formulated the event in his introduction to the *Actes du tribunal révolutionnaire*: "Six weeks after [his triumph before the revolutionary tribunal], the murderous hand of a *Maraticized* woman would strike him dead."[18] So the woman is not the *author* of the crime, she is reduced to a hand; guided by whom? Marat himself, answers Walter. The idea is correct in the sense that Charlotte Corday responded to Marat's appeals for blood with a bloody act—even if Marat had certainly not had himself in mind! But the fundamental, undeniable difference by which Charlotte Corday definitively constituted herself a heroine was her passage to the act. Charlotte Corday, in that age of emphatic words, rhetorical excess, journalistic hysteria (see, for example, the litanies of insults in the "grandes colères" of Père Duchesne) believed only in the deed. As a Stoic, she mistrusted words and privileged the deed that spoke for itself, definitively, with no need for commentary. She was from this point of view a living illustration of that revolutionary ideology which, verbally, forever repeated the primacy of the deed over speech. Her action, fully justified in her own eyes, did not contradict Saint-Just's lapidary order: "Animate virtue with the dexterity of crime against crime."[19] It was her rigor and integrity that made Charlotte Corday intolerable to the revolutionaries. That is why it was not enough to get rid of her physically; it had to appear that she had never existed.

For the painter David, pushing Charlotte Corday beyond the frame of his painting was magic enough to erase her. But it was harder to manipulate the real. Unable to deny Charlotte Corday's existence, the Jacobins struggled to deform her image. Fearing the exemplary value of her act and the charismatic effect of her youth and beauty, they posted across the city a text decrying the assassin's great ugliness. "This woman being called pretty was not pretty at all; she was a *virago*, chubby rather than fresh, slovenly, as female philosophers and sharp thinkers almost always are . . . Moreover, this remark would be pointless were it not generally true that any pretty woman who enjoys being pretty clings to life and fears death, . . . Her head was stuffed with all sorts of books; she declared, or rather she confessed with an affectation bordering on the ridiculous, that she had read everything from Tacitus to the *Portier des Chartreux*. . . . All these things mean that this woman had hurled herself completely outside of her sex" (Sunday, July 21, Year II of the French Republic).[20]

In his *Discours aux mânes de Marat et Le Pelletier*, Sade eloquently took up the accusation that Charlotte Corday was outside her sex. "Marat's barbarous assassin, like those mixed beings whose sex is impossible to determine, vomited up from hell to the despair of both sexes, directly belongs to neither."[21] The solemnity required by the genre of the eulogy prevented libertine excesses; transgressing her sex, Charlotte Corday became an unsexed monster. In the erotic universe of the Sadean novel, in contrast, transgression leads to the triumph of sexuality. "Oh! what an excess of wickedness!" sighs Juliette when she begins to love La Durand, an androgynous monster endowed with a clitoris "as long as a finger."[22] But in the Revolution's morality androgyny and wickedness do not stimulate sighs of desire. And Sade was too gifted a rhetorician to use the wrong style!

Thus, when Charlotte Corday asked in her final request for the services of a painter ("since I still have a few moments to live, might I hope, citizens, that you will allow me to have myself painted"[23]), the reason was neither coquettishness nor self-pity. We should instead read here an effort to counteract the annihilation process denying that she was the author of her act (an attitude her judges had no trouble reconciling with the verdict that she was guilty of that very act) and an attempt to stand up against the systematic deformation of her appearance. In Charlotte Corday, the will to survive led only in an accessory way to the fragile and imperfect form of a sketch. The portrait was not intended for anyone near. There was no privileged preserver of her image. The memory she wanted to reach was History's, an impersonal realm she had to attain and mark for eternity. And she had to do so through a single deed, with no way—in contrast to what happens with intersubjective memory—to establish the base of preliminary interiorisation formed by a thousand successive impressions. Charlotte Corday assumed the totality of her act for all eternity. She wanted to be sculpted by a single blow.

Marat's partisans saw in Charlotte Corday a monster to be wiped off the face of the earth. The gesture of the executioner slapping her lifeless head is sufficiently expressive of the inexpiable nature of her crime. But what did those who admired her, those for whom her act was an unequaled exploit, see in her? They recognized in Charlotte Corday the inspired and coldly fanatic reader of Plutarch's *Parallel Lives*. They bowed before what seemed to them a model of heroism. André Chénier wrote in his ode to Marie-Anne-Charlotte Corday:

> La vertu seule est libre. Honneur de notre histoire,
> Notre immortel opprobre y vit avec ta gloire,
> Seule tu fus un homme, et vengeas les humains.

Et nous, eunuques vils, troupeau lâche sans âme,
Nous savons répéter quelques plaintes de femme,
Mais le fer pèserait à nos débiles mains.

From condemnation to admiration, Charlotte Corday went from unspeakable monstrosity to the very incarnation of the virile ideal. She was admired as a heroic *woman* only by other exceptional women, like Madame Roland.

2

Madame Roland learned of Marat's assassination in prison. She had been arrested on June 1, 1793. Incarcerated in the Abbaye, she wrote letter after letter complaining that her arrest was illegal. To attenuate the illegality, she was freed on the morning of June 24 and arrested again that evening, this time according to all the proper procedures. She was sent to Sainte-Pélagie, where she would remain until her death; found guilty November 8, she was executed that same day. She at first considered taking as her lawyer Chauveau-Lagarde, who had been the attorney for Charlotte Corday and the queen. But he agreed with her final decision to write her own defense and read it to the court. She was silenced as soon as she began to speak.

Even if it is due only to chance, there is in Madame Roland's proximity to Charlotte Corday the concrete and physical fact that the two were confined in the same Abbaye cell at an interval of a few weeks. This cell was a dirty, foul-smelling *petit cabinet*, but it had the advantage of holding only one inmate at a time. Madame Roland had books and flowers brought into the cell. The guard told her that he would from then on call it the "Pavillon de Flore." "I was unaware," wrote Madame Roland, "that he was at that very moment intending it for Brissot, whom I did not know to be inside; that soon afterwards it would be inhabited by a heroine worthy of a better age, the famous *Corday*. . . . "[24] On a more profound level, Madame Roland's fate was linked to Charlotte Corday's in the sense that the latter's murder, which everyone was trying to paint as the effect of a Girondist conspiracy, worsened the former's situation before revolutionary opinion. Madame Roland was convinced of Charlotte Corday's total independence: "The effect of this death was what the Right had foreseen, and that is another reason to be confident that the fugitives are not the instigators of Marat's assassination, *even were it not absurd to suppose one could command the resolution of a Corday*."[25]

Madame Roland did not accept the conspiracy hypothesis, not only because violence and murder were outside the character of the Girondists, whom Madame Roland called "enemies of blood," but also because she was familiar with Charlotte Corday's heroic ideal. This familiarity came not from a shared project but from the readings common to the two women, both of whom caught fire on encountering, through the Ancients and Rousseau, an ideal republic, a Stoic concept of life, and above all a Stoic concept of death. Stoic wisdom, an ethic of asceticism, was built on a division of the world into *what depends on us* and *what does not depend on us*. Stoicism consists of refusing to suffer and exhaust oneself through passions that are pointless because they are directed toward things beyond one's reach.

Freedom is conceived as an internal space on which the external world has no purchase. The philosopher can therefore remain calm under torture, can be free in prison. Charlotte Corday and Madame Roland saw their incarceration as a way to test their Stoic indifference to the accidents of fate. "I'm in good shape in my prison," the first declared, whereas Madame Roland said she lived in the Abbaye or Sainte-Pélagie exactly the same way she lived at home, by eating a frugal diet and devoting all her time to study and writing. With her usual vigilant intelligence, Madame Roland saw that Stoicism was a matter of method. "Firmness consists not only of raising oneself above circumstances through an effort of will but also of remaining above circumstances through suitable behavior and care. Wisdom is composed of all the acts useful in its conservation and exercise."[26] As one of those with wisdom, Madame Roland observed a strict schedule divided into hours spent learning English (through reading Shaftesbury and Thompson), drawing (a talent closely bound up with her childhood; her father was a master engraver, and Madame Roland studied his art with him) and, last and most important, writing her *Mémoires*. Unlike Charlotte Corday, who became famous through an act as brief as it was fatal—to herself as well as her victim—it is through writing that the memory of Madame Roland has come down to us. Madame Roland is not a cold, enigmatic marble sculpture but a speaking presence, a voice. Michelet said this about her: "Madame Roland, Robespierre . . . both have the same quirk: they were always writing, they were born scribes."[27] This "quirk" showed itself completely when Madame Roland was in prison, even if she had already written a huge amount as an adolescent:

letters to a friend, thoughts, curious literary exercises in which
she would compose sermons for pleasure.

All her life, however, Madame Roland fought against this
passion. She denied being a woman writer. Her judgement of
such creatures was critical: "Never did I feel the slightest
temptation to be a writer one day."[28] And to a friend who
predicted such a future for her, "Mademoiselle, there's no use
denying it, you'll end up writing a work!" she gave this reply:
"Then it will be under the name of someone else . . . I'd chew off
my fingers before becoming a writer."[29] It took the nearness of
death for Madame Roland to renounce so strict a prohibition (or
so brutal a castration); she needed to feel that, as she put it, the
hours were spurring her on.[30] She authorized herself to write only
under cover of a testamentary act. Earlier, her marriage with
Monsieur Roland de la Platrière allowed her to write *under the
name of someone else*. Her union with Roland, who was much
older than his wife, had nothing to do with sensuality but
completely satisfied her need for the studious life.[31] With him,
she could continue to live in the company of Plutarch and the
philosophers dear to her. He was suited to her through
intellectual affinities. Madame Roland loved and esteemed her
husband for his knowledge. She was closely associated with his
work as an Encyclopedist. Moreover, as she wrote, Roland made
her "his copyist and his proof corrector."[32] When her husband
became Minister of the Interior in 1792, their association did not
end. On the contrary: impassioned by politics, she took part in
all he did and certainly influenced him as well. In her *Mémoires*,
Madame Roland continuously refers to herself as a wife, insisting
on her secondary role. "I knew the role that suited my sex, and I
never abandoned it."[33] In reality, even when performing the
modest duties of a secretary, she constantly betrayed in practice
the place of a wife she strove to defend in theory. Remembering a
letter to the pope composed by her but signed by the Minister
Roland, she noted, with amusement: "The pleasure of these
contrasts was in the secrecy itself." And she added, in her defense,
"But the only singular thing in all this is its rarity; why should a
woman not serve as her husband's secretary without reducing his
merit? Everyone knows ministers cannot do everything by
themselves, and this much is certain: if the wives of ministers
under the old or even the new regime had been able to prepare
letters, circulars or posters, they would have been much better off
spending their time doing so instead of petitioning or plotting
for the sake of everybody they knew."[34]

All those declarations of modesty were useless. Her personality was too strong, her intelligence too keen, her political ambition too intense for her role to remain hidden from public view. As much as, if not more than her husband, she was the sans-culottes' target and the object of attacks from Marat and Père Duchesne. "The pamphlets have multiplied," she wrote in a letter, "and I doubt more horrors have been published against Marie Antoinette; they're comparing me to her and calling me by one of her names every day. I'm Galigai, Brinvilliers, Voisin, everything monstrous imaginable, and the market women want to treat me like Madame Lamballe."[35] This last woman, after being decapitated, had her body cut apart and her sex removed. As a joke, someone made a mustache of her "virginal part," as a horrified Mercier put it.

This litany of the names of bad women, which was in revolutionary rhetoric a constant counterpoint to the line of great men, the heroes of Greece and the Roman Republic, did not impress Madame Roland for the very good reason that she modeled herself on the great men. She had no choice. As Paule-Marie Duhet analysed the situation, "Women as a group had no 'historic reminiscences' to which to refer. Too often they mentioned, as if to give themselves courage, the name of some famous woman: one name, which is to say an exception. But nothing allowed them to find those attitudes, that phraseology giving a group the calm assurance of its cohesion, and thereby guaranteeing it successes from which its cohesion will emerge with greater strength. The most intelligent, most cultivated women, like Etta Palm, spoke of imitating the virtues and patriotism of Roman ladies. But as a matter of fact, how do you behave like a Roman lady?"[36]

Madame Roland would therefore behave to the end like a Roman *man*. There is a story that, on the road to her execution, when people screamed "To the guillotine!" she answered simply, "I'm on my way."

The *savoir-mourir* demonstrated to a supreme degree by Charlotte Corday and Madame Roland—basing themselves on a morality intrinsic to the revolutionary ideal—was frightful in the eyes of those who condemned them. The *Moniteur Universel* combines Marie-Antoinette, Olympe de Gouges and Madame Roland in a single article of censure. "Marie-Antoinette . . . was a bad mother, a debauched wife, and she died under the curses of those she wanted to destroy. . . . Olympe de Gouges, born with an exalted imagination, took her delirium for an inspiration of nature . . . The Roland woman, a fine mind for great plans, a philosopher on note paper, the queen of a moment . . . was a monster however you look at her, . . . Even though she was a mother, she had sacrificed nature by trying to raise herself above it; the desire to be learned led her to forget the virtues of her sex, and that always-dangerous forgetting finally led to her death on the guillotine" ("To Republican Women," November 19, 1793).[37]

These women had to be doubly condemned for a double treachery: they were counter-revolutionaries and they were imitation women. In putting them to death, society did nothing more than get rid of what Nature itself had discarded. Such "severity" is explained by the very new threat posed by women like Madame Roland, who wanted to participate openly in political life, who were no longer content with drawing-room intrigues. More generally, the post-mortem moral condemnation of women who set a bad example can be understood through the particularly moving theatricality, the romantic seduction attached to the death of a woman. A young man named Adam Lux, author of a thesis on enthusiasm, fell in love with Charlotte Corday for her exceptional deed and her strength before punishment. After seeing her die, his sole desire was to follow her into death. Haunted by her "unique and immortal memory,"[38] he was guillotined five months later.

Michelet, in an astonishing formula used during arguments on the reactionary character of female actions, announces that a woman's death is always "impolitic."[39] Impolitic, no doubt. Apolitical, certainly not. This is the scandal of the executions of women who, deprived of political rights, were nevertheless executed for political errors—a scandal pointed out by Olympe de Gouges in her *Declaration of the Rights of Woman*, dedicated to Marie-Antoinette, in a statement of feminist alliance beyond political divisions. "No one should be disturbed for opinions, no matter how basic; woman has the right to be guillotined; she must also have the right to be heard, provided she does not disturb the public order established by Law."[40]

Unlike Olympe de Gouges, Charlotte Corday and Madame Roland made no feminist demands. Instead they took up positions squarely on the terrain of men's thought and action, and there they proved to be daunting rivals in full command of virtues assumed to be exclusively masculine: Charlotte Corday showed herself to be unsurpassable in the rigor and extremism of her deed; Madame Roland, even to the most unsympathetic eyes, was exceptional in her intelligence, her culture, and the intensity of her political passion. Both women chose their course not as a provocation (that would have been less serious because it was another way to give public opinion its due) but because they were driven by an inner logic, by past readings, solitude and reflection. They had a religious and philosophical formation that made them fervent Stoics, Rousseauists and republicans. This means that they accepted in every way the ideology and morals of the Revolution—except that that did not submit to the role it assigned to them. This role was too modest, too withdrawn; it gave too little cause for enthusiasm and showed no way to secure a life (or a death) worthy of the models described by Plutarch. And that is what they desired, with neither ambivalence nor hesitation; they were ready for the heightened heroism such a choice implied, and they were determined to stand against the condemnations it was bound to provoke.

To the rigorous self-transcendence necessary in every heroic action, women had to add the supplementary violence of casting themselves "outside their sex." They risked their lives on a stage that gave them in exchange neither power nor gratitude. They burned themselves *for nothing* in the flame of the Revolution. And when, overcoming all obstacles, they raised themselves to the level of courage and heroism of a Brutus, they were only chided for not staying at home—which was after all what they were supposed to do.

NOTES

1. Jules Michelet, *Les Femmes de la Révolution* (Paris, 1854), 26.
2. Ibid., 53.
3. Diderot, in his text entitled *Sur les femmes*, writes this about them: "Impenetrable in dissimulation, cruel in vengeance, constant in their projects, without scruples as to the means of success, animated by a deep and secret hatred for male despotism, women seem to be engaged in a facile conspiracy to dominate, a kind of league like that among the priests of all nations" (*OEuvres complètes* [Paris, 1951] 950-51).
4. Michelet, *Les Femmes*, 303.
5. Quoted by Paule-Marie Duhet in her *Les Femmes et la Révolution* (Paris, 1971), 105-06.
6. Ibid., 106.
7. Madame Roland, *Lettres*, ed. Claude Perroud (Paris, 1902), 512.
8. Michelet, *Les Femmes*, 198.
9. Jean-Jacques Rousseau, *Les Confessions* (Paris, 1958), 1:47.
10. Madame Roland, *Mémoires* (Paris, 1986), 212-13.
11. Gérard Walter, ed. *Actes du Tribunal Révolutionnaire* (Paris, 1968), 20.

12. *Adresse de la veuve J.P. Marat, l'Ami du peuple, à la Convention nationale,* Paris, ed. Archives parlementaires, 19 juillet, 1793.

13. *Adresse de la Société des Républicaines Révolutionnaires.* Paris, ed. Archives Parel Parlementaires, 17 juillet, 1793.

14. Walter, *Actes du Tribunal,* 20.

15. Archives nationales, F7 4385, no. 4.

16. Walter, *Actes du Tribunal,* 22.

17. Gilbert Lascault, *Figurées, défigurées: Petit vocabulaire de la féminité représentée* (Paris, 1977), 36.

18. Walter, *Actes du Tribunal,* 10.

19. Saint-Just, *Oeuvres* (Paris, 1946), 116.

20. Cf. the collection of the Fonds Lacassagne.

21. D.A.F. de Sade, *Oeuvres complètes* (Paris, 1966), 8:287.

22. Sade, *Oeuvres,* 6:67.

23. Walter, *Actes du Tribunal,* 29.

24. Roland, *Mémoires,* 176.

25. Ibid., 361; Emphasis added.

26. Ibid., 180.

27. Michelet, *Les Femmes,* 163.

28. Roland, *Mémoires,* 305.

29. Ibid., 321.

30. Ibid., 328.

31. "I entered marriage for serious and rational purposes," Madame Roland wrote elegantly, "and I found no reason to change my attitude." *Mémoires,* 332.

32. Ibid., 333.

33. Ibid., 63.

34. Ibid., 305.

35. Roland, *Lettres,* 445.

36. Duhet, *Les Femmes,* 217.

37. Quoted by Duhet, *Les Femmes,* 205.

38. Walter, *Actes du Tribunal,* 37.

39. Michelet, *Les Femmes,* 217.

40. Olympe de Gouges, *Oeuvres* (Paris), 104.

DISORDER/ORDER: REVOLUTIONARY ART AS PERFORMATIVE REPRESENTATION

James H. Rubin

Here writing becomes like a signature placed at the bottom of a collective proclamation. . . .
—Roland Barthes, "Political Writing," *Writing Degree Zero*

Although something known as the Revolution undeniably existed and was the condition for an art that can properly be called Revolutionary, it may be futile to seek a single definition of either.[1] However, some distinctions are nonetheless useful for an understanding of the Revolutionary role of art. First, we can separate work that merely happened to be made during the Revolutionary period from art that responds directly to political circumstances. And within such directly political art, we can distinguish between "Revolutionary art" and "Revolutionary imagery," the latter as found in popular prints, on official documents, and on utilitarian objects. Though there was significant cross-fertilization between the two, I shall focus here on works in which visual configuration not only responds to but in some sense helps create the Revolutionary experience. If we grant that the Revolution is a "signified" of such art, we can treat Revolutionary art as the Revolution's representation.

It is often noted that the word "revolution" is metaphorical, implying the overturn of the past, a turning point, or even a "re-turn" to a new beginning. It contains a sense both of the unprecedented and yet of the search for an original or ultimate truth, of the breaking down of one order and of the creation of a new one.[2] I will suggest that Revolutionary art embodies this dialectic of disorder and order: in both responding to and creating the Revolution's ideals and its daily reality, its representational strategies embody the Revolutionary process.

Thus narrowly considered, Revolutionary art is *performative*. An explanation of this term taken from linquistics and of my particular use of it will be helpful. J.L. Austin's *How to do Things with Words* was first to use the dual concepts of constative/performative.[3] A constative statement describes or reports, whereas for phrases such as "I say," "I bet," "I swear" or "I promise," the saying of the words constitutes "part of the

doing of an action not normally described as saying something."[4]
Austin emphasizes that a performative depends on conventional
acceptance for its authority. My use of the term is particular for
two reasons. First, in figurative art, separation between constative
and performative is not always clear, since all visual representation purports to be descriptive. The degree to which a
representation refers to its maker may determine the degree to
which it is performative. Austin notes that "I dedicate" is a
performative and that written utterances or inscriptions can be
rendered performative by appending a signature.[5] Second, what I
will call the "revolutionary performative" has a radically different
relationship to convention from that of Austin's performative.
Revolutionary performative depends on convention as what it
necessarily *violates* for the production of new conventions. On
the most basic level, violation or rupture itself becomes the new
convention for the Revolutionary audience and hence a mark of
patriotism for the performer. Revolutionary art is necessarily
divisive.

Examples of this kind of Revolutionary art are exceptional
rather than the rule—the Academy trained artists to avoid the
unprecedented. Of course, illustrations of contemporary events,
battle scenes, festivals and so on abound, especially in prints, but
also in some paintings, as in the projects for the Year II.[6] Scenes
of dynamic collective action, such as Fulcran-Jean Harriet's
Blacksmiths at the Convention (fig. 1), reflect the intensity of
Revolutionary challenges to established order. Their composition-
ally dispersed figure groups at extremes of action or emotion
typify a common Revolutionary dramatic formula. Moreover, the
dominance of realism in such productions certainly signifies
another form of disorder—the "real" as inherently disorderly—as
well as a new artistic order, in which the modern is pre-eminent.[7]
But the basic relationship of form and content they reveal is not
fundamentally different from illustrations of earlier history or of
non-political events.

In addition, many painters continued the tradition of using
narrative subjects from classical history, relying for political
legibility on associations between their themes and the present.
David's *Brutus* (fig. 2), which shows the Roman consul after the
execution of his sons for treason, is a fine example of a father's
devotion to the state despite his personal loyalties. Composed in
the summer of 1789, the picture was re-exhibited in 1791, recent
political events having made its patriotic ideals all the more

FIGURE 1. Fulcran-Jean Harriet, *The Blacksmiths at the Convention, during the Festival of Saltpeter, 30 Ventôse, Year II*, 1794, Drawing, Paris, Musée Carnavalet. Reproduced by permission.

pertinent.[8] A second example is *The Death of Caius Gracchus*, by the Babouvist student of David and member of the Revolutionary tribunal, Jean-Baptiste Topino-Lebrun. It was displayed at the Salon of 1798, just after the execution of Gracchus Babeuf.[9] However, these pictures, which more or less bracket the Revolution chronologically, again deploy traditional pictorial vehicles, however strained. Their potentially inflammatory ideas are couched in the allusion of Neo-Classicism rather than in a direct Revolutionary discourse, as I shall argue later. I focus here on two more innovative examples of Revolutionary art that better embody attempts to achieve effective pictorial form for the representation of Revolutionary power. My examples are Jacques-Louis David's *Marat Assassinated* of 1793 (fig. 3) and Jean-Baptiste Regnault's *Liberty or Death* of 1794 (fig. 4). Created during the Terror, when the Revolution was at its point of greatest urgency and rupture with the past, these pictures, whose differences suggest poles for Revolutionary representation, none-theless reveal shared responses to its conditions.[10] Both are

FIGURE 2. Jacques-Louis David, *Lictors Returning the Bodies of Brutus' Sons*, 1789, oil on canvas, Paris, Musée du Louvre. Reproduced by permission.

engaged in a pictorial and ideological struggle to bring forth images of order from a disastrously disorderly world. Both are ideologically divisive.

This paper views Revolutionary art as that in which the mode of representation of the Revolution is an act of Revolution and refers to itself as such. My argument for Revolutionary art might echo the French title of Austin's book, *Quand dire, c'est faire* (when saying is doing). I hold here that Revolutionary art occurs when, so to speak, "representing the Revolution is making the Revolution," that is, when "I represent the Revolution" can be taken in both its pictorial ("I paint the Revolution") and its ideological ("My action is [representative of] the Revolution") meanings. Revolutionary art, though it may use previous conventions as a foil, violates them to establish new ones as a means of addressing and shaping a new audience.

I have chosen my two primary examples not only because of their paradigmatic status for the concept of the revolutionary performative in art, but for the polarity they suggest in the identity of the performer and his relationship to that audience. The *Marat* and the *Liberty or Death* represent two genres

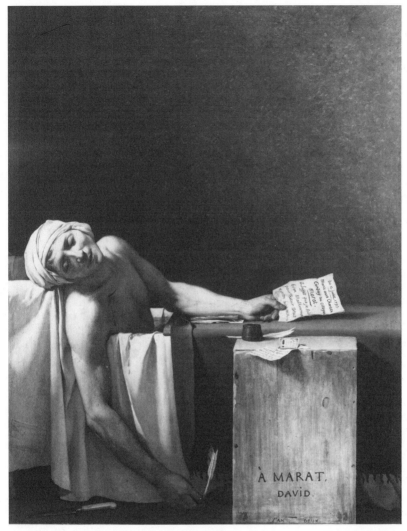

FIGURE 3. David, *Marat Assassinated*, 1793, oil on canvas, Brussels, Musée Royal des Beaux-Arts. Reproduced by permission.

encouraged by the Revolution: contemporary history painting and allegory. They may imply two sometimes contradictory concepts of the Revolution: the historical and the ideological. Under the Ancien Régime, power was represented in the person of the King, in whom the power of representation was vested through the patronage system.[11] In contrast, the Revolution was

FIGURE 4. Jean-Baptiste Regnault, *Liberty or Death*, 1793, oil on canvas, Hamburg, Kunsthalle. Reproduced by permission.

founded, sometimes unrealistically, both on a sense of community of interest among individuals (however diversely defined) and on abstract ideas. The two principal areas of visual culture from which Revolutionary art drew reflect these dualities. The most obvious were the great public festivals. More than just a means of indoctrination, such gatherings created the kind of collective experience essential to the formation of a culture, especially one claiming to be new. As Mona Ozouf writes, "the legislator made laws for the people; the festivals made people for the laws."[12]

David's program for the Festival of Unity and Indivisibility of the Republic especially abounds in ritual bonding ceremonies.[13] Second, the Revolutionary bureaucracy generated reams of archives, official documents, and public announcements. Many of these were decorated or illustrated with emblematic or symbolic characters that paralleled, highlighted, or framed their verbal content. I argue that the written word was a paradigm for Revolutionary representation. Symbols such as the Phrygian bonnet, the level, or the fasces referred to concepts primarily understood through words (Liberty, Equality, Fraternity). Moreover, the festivals were themselves founded on such concepts, so that their scenarios employed the sequentiality of narrative and the formality of declamation.[14]

Beyond their obvious differences, the *Marat* and the *Liberty or Death* partake of both the popular and the verbal elements of these sources, yet without relying on narrativity. They are like fragments from such ensembles, displaying abstracted and frontal structures one might describe as hieroglyphic or emblematic, while depending upon the same codes of signification. Their unique concentration and intensity, stretched between the confrontational and the meditative, give them an independence that distinguishes them from ordinary Revolutionary art. They reflect both the classical ambitions of high culture and the Revolution's pressing need for art to go beyond the *exemplum virtutis*—to become performative. In seeking the legibility and abstraction of the word and the immediacy of the emblem, their visual formulation responds to a need for order and comprehensibility in the Revolution itself. Hence, they also harbor undercurrents of coercion and stress linked to Revolutionary disorder and violence. Though too extreme to engender a new style, they are powerful prototypes of a new psychology. They reverse the classical position of an art reflecting the mind of the observer, embodying and confirming the conventions and assumptions of its audience's ideology. That ideology was in disarray. Rather, they imply instead two radically new positions: the appropriation of representation by the individual and the transformation of the viewer by this new standpoint. Unlike religious propaganda, this art places its audience in a position of discomfort, as if it were being interpellated by images more real than itself.[15] The Revolutionary artist converts the picture plane from a transparent opening onto a simulacrum of reality to a platform for political projection.

David's Marat: Representation/Self-Presentation

The foremost figure in the visual arts during the Revolution was the painter Jacques-Louis David. Before 1789 his art already had a potentially political disposition; the Revolution saw that content emerge from behind the mask of classicism to become progressively radicalized.[16] David became a militant, practicing the Enlightenment ideal of art as propaganda.[17] His activities ranged from producing anti-English caricatures and designs for Revolutionary dress to organizing Revolutionary festivals and new institutions for artists. As a député and member of the Committees of General Security and Public Instruction, David was at the peak of his power during the Terror.[18] More than any other work, the *Marat Assassinated*[19] exemplifies the Revolutionary inseparability of artistic activity and political life.

When the *Marat* was exhibited in the courtyard of the Louvre, according to the sole surviving account, "its effect was so terrifying that it was difficult to stand the sight of it for long."[20] Its power derived from a dual grounding in historical reality and pictorial tradition. David's personal association with and sympathy for the ideas of Jean-Paul Marat were legion. Marat was one of those who toward the end of 1792 had proposed David's candacy to the Convention.[21] Several months later, responding to a verbal attack on Marat before its assembled members, David rushed to the journalist's side shouting: "I demand that you assassinate me; I too am a virtuous man. Liberty will triumph!"[22] These strangely violent, disconnected and prophetic words not only reveal the depth of David's identification with his subject-to-be, they illuminate the painting's disruptive expressive structure. In early 1793, David had organized a public funeral for Lepeletier de Saint-Fargeau and made a commemorative painting dedicated to the victim (fig. 5). So immediately on learning of Marat's murder by Charlotte Corday on July 13, 1793, the Convention turned not just to Marat's friend, nor merely to the outstanding painter of the time, but to someone already rehearsed in creating propaganda imagery. David's famous answer to the official request was an emphatic: "Je le ferai!" He organized Marat's funeral procession on July 16 as well.

It has often been demonstrated that the *Marat* has a dual character as "reportage and epitaph": it combines historical and funerary imagery.[23] Of course, David's mise-en-scène was rooted in Marat's biography. Marat suffered from leprosy and spent hours in the bath. David claimed to have seen him there the

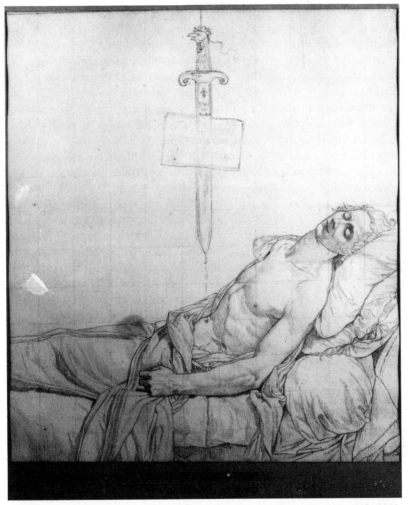

FIGURE 5. Anatole Devosge, after J.L. David, *Lepeletier Assassinated*, 1793, Drawing, Dijon, Musée des Beaux-Arts. Reproduced by permission.

previous night, and only the rapid putrefaction of his body prevented him from displaying it before burial in the position he chose for him in the painting. Charlotte Corday used false pretenses to obtain her fatal audience. The note David placed in Marat's hand is true to the spirit of her disguise, though its wording considerably simplifies the original.[24] The draft on Marat's writing box offering a monetary note to a soldier's widow may derive from his efforts of June 4, 1793, to aid the families of combatants, though no such letter has actually been found.[25] Details such as the bloody bathwater, the knife wound, the bare room, the simple crate and the paper money are credible. On the one hand, the painting could appear, so to speak, "styleless." It seems totally devoted to the referent: nothing artistic, that is, of purely aesthetic value denoting the artist's personal creativity, is obvious in the anatomy, posture, lighting, details, or setting.[26] David thus broke decisively with previous traditions of high art. This is an image "written" in the passive voice: history *is represented*, as if it had *presented* itself. Obviously, such an image's propaganda value lies in its claim to be objective. Only the signature, as we shall see, reveals its subjective source. Of course, historical hindsight enables us to see that David has intensified and manipulated reality for the sake of dramatic effect and clarity: he has skillfully arranged the light and background to set the figure off; the wound ("blessure *sacrilège*," for Baudelaire) and Marat's limp arm resemble Christ's; he has certainly made Marat's quarters more Spartan than they really were; and there are knowledgable allusions to antiquity. What is important, then, is that David's audience was ready to read his picture as a convincing record of truth; it assumed his art to be an unmanipulated record of fact. Thus the terror the painting inspired was the terror of reality itself. Horror at the evidence of violence, and fear of more in revenge, were the inseparable responses to Marat's death.[27]

In preserving its subject's appearance, funerary art responds to the instinctive urge to deny death.[28] In casting its subject's disappearance in explicable and comforting terms, religious art gives death a purpose. David evoked both Christian pietà and deathbed scenes of ancient warriors. At a time of political tension, this duality embodied a call to Revolutionary unity, with religious overtones appealing to the people and the reincarnation of antiquity playing to the intellectual and historical ambitions of the Convention.[29] The painting directly recalled the *Lepeletier*, which, like the *Marat*, evoked the public funeral David had organized. Both subjects were paired as martyrs to liberty, as at the ceremony of David's *section* during which the painter presented the *Marat* to the Convention. Both works were hung over a pair of sarcophagi in the Louvre courtyard, under a temporary chapel-like structure.[30] The *Marat* is thus associated with the cult that began with veneration of the victim's heart at the former Eglise des Cordeliers.[31] It was an emblem affirming the message of other public manifestations placing Marat's death in the orderly context of sacrifice for a sacred cause.[32]

But it is easy to see that.David's homage to Marat goes far beyond the call of duty to the Republic. For one thing, by naming Marat through the dedicatory words, "A MARAT," David also named himself as mourner, as his painting's audience. By making the painting a public ex-voto, David made it refer to a personal relationship with Marat; he gave himself a "presence" in the picture ostensibly offered to Marat. For another, David's celebration at his *section* meeting of the picture's completion and his speech to the Convention on the occasion of its delivery emphasize a personal act of donation.[33] Finally, the painting's illusionism claims for it a physical presence in the realm of tangible reality. David produced the sensation not only of historical reality but of an object in the round; the painting reads not just as historical and funerary portrait, but as votive stele. Its gravestone-like shape and the inscription-like block lettering of the dedication and signature imply the thickness of a slab; the unfinished background above the figure recalls the roughness of backgrounds in many sculpted reliefs.

These characteristics produce multiple effects. Visually merging the background and the canvas surface, David projects Marat forward into the viewer's space much as would occur on a tombstone. He "re-enacts" Marat's funeral, displaying the body in the bathtub the way he originally wanted. In creating the image of a Marat continuous with the viewer's own physical existence, David affords the psychological experience of the subject's historical congruence with the real world. He reminds us that the salvation for which this "Jacobin Christ" acted was for the present. But at the same time, historical immediacy is contradicted by the very device that helps create the physical response: the painting's character as votive monument. Viewed as the latter, the painting is experienced as durable object and as personal memorial. The dedicatory signature is a reminder that the painting/object remains in David's "possession."

The signature is one of several allusions to or instances of writing in the picture. The man who declared that France would establish a new order solely through the power of its philosophy had been murdered while performing the act of writing. The didactic contrast between two instruments of action—quill and knife—is dramatized by juxtaposition in the foreground. A similar contrast may be inferred from a comparison between the

two painted texts: Marat's charitable request versus Charlotte
Corday's written deception. In addition to their realist purpose,
the wordings in these documents permit the kind of clarity
usually associated with prints illustrating historical events. David
has introduced a kind of historical commentary without
destroying realist illusion.[34] In this second reading, the image is
"written" in the active voice. More than an anonymous painter-
craftsman executing imagery called for by society, David is donor,
audience (mourner), and commentator.

These coexisting readings can be stated as follows: Marat is
represented; David represents Marat. They correspond to the
distinction between constative and performative speech. But
David has transgressed the bounds of classical representation.
According to the observer from the Louvre courtyard I quoted
earlier, the extreme effects produced by David's works could only
be explained by politics: "The expression of horror in these two
portraits [the *Marat* and the *Lepeletier*] permeates both their
ensemble and their details, proving that in addition to the artist's
virile and skilled touch he must be inflamed by an ardent love of
country."[35] Hence, to produce the effect of reality, the artist must
be inspired by patriotism. His ideals are signified by an artistic
performance which appropriates representation as a system from
some "objective" realm to that of the individual, who is also a
member of a collectivity. Objectivity resides in the individual.
Though the *Marat* appears unmediated, that is precisely the sign
of David's artistic presence. Linking our readings together: David
represents himself representing Marat. Through patriotism, he
becomes a representation of the Revolution representing itself.

Identifying with Marat, taking his and Marat's acts as his
subjects, David represents the Revolution as self-realization. His
representations, hanging in the Convention's meeting hall,
constitute a history prominently displayed, performed and
authorized (made performative) by signature, visually and
oratorically, in the very place where law was made (and signed).
Yet the obverse is present, too: the funerary image with its
gruesome details and its confrontational presence harbors an
undercurrent of violence. Self-realization takes its toll. Despite the
painting's call to order, David's viewers were disconcerted both by
its too present evidence of disorder and—our Louvre observer
implied—by its austere imposition of order (as well as perhaps by
David's own too passionate performances). Despite its rigor, the
Marat's dualities recall David's demand to be assassinated. Both

are disruptive and disjunctive, indicative and imperative; transitions are missing, as in expletives; they are emblematic and unmitigated by artistic license. A brilliant effort to make sense of Revolutionary disorder, the *Marat* nevertheless was all too like the Revolution—by 1793, both compelling and beyond control.

REGNAULT'S LIBERTY OR DEATH: MISE-EN-PAGE/MISE-EN-SCÈNE

In trying to give form to its history, the Revolution looked to a series of writing acts, as if they embodied rationality. Indeed, David's *Oath of the Tennis Court*, the first major project for a painting of Revolutionary history, depicts the oath of delegates of the Third Estate not to disband before writing a constitution. Constituting itself through a written document, the Revolution gave itself the sense of order and durability. The painting's balance between the dual themes of collective action and ideology may reflect the complexity of the delegates' task. Its combination of realism and symmetrical design, and of dramatic unity despite strictly individuated figures, looks to the illustrative character of early Revolutionary images while initiating a process of reduction and emblematization.[36]

If writing was the Revolution's central representational activity, its obsession with language is understandable.[37] In his *Histoire de la langue française*, Brunot divides the effects of the Revolution on language into phases which build up and then back away from the rigorous and compulsory linguistic practices of the Terror.[38] In 1789, *Les Révolutions de Paris* asserted that "we should not forget in this revolution the powerful effect of the language of symbols."[39] In the midst of the Terror, Robespierre declared before the Jacobin Club that "nothing is more contrary to the interests of the people and equality than being difficult with language."[40] Revolutionary iconoclasm is well known.[41] In 1794, after destroying church images and ornaments, the Société Populaire of Condom declared: "May speech [la parole] from now on be our sole instrument."[42] In art, the structural result of the dominance of the word was emblematic flattening, eschewing narrative and denying escape toward an ideal or imaginary realm behind the picture plane. Our two examples present simple designs and project painted forms foward sculpturally to structure the viewer's world. Ideas were codified through a kind of "hieroglyphic" system, in which visual signs had the clarity of the word. And in one extreme case, a statue of the Republic projected by David, inscriptions at various places on its surface

FIGURE 6. Villeneuve, *View of the Six Different Stations of the Festival of the Unity and Indivisibility of the Republic (10 August, 1793)*, 1793, engraving, Paris, Bibliothèque Nationale, Cabinet des Estampes, Collection De Vinck, No. 6171. Reproduced by permission.

were to decode it, and hence the Republic as its referent, as an assemblage of verbal concepts.[43]

The use of conventional concept-symbols arranged in familiar patterns constitutes a non-verbal form of writing. As organizer of Revolutionary festivals, David was a professional manipulator of ideological texts and symbolic images. One has only to glance at illustrations of the Festival of Unity and Indivisibility of the Republic (August 10, 1793) to discover his fluency with the allegorical apparatus (fig. 6).[44] Paintings like the *Marat* and the *Lepeletier* can be grouped with images like *Liberty* (fig. 7) and *Republican France Offering her Breasts* (fig. 8) for their immediacy linked to emblematic simplicity and forward projection. While the latter make no pretense of referring to historical events, they were a part of everyday life, omnipresent on Revolutionary monuments and pervasive on documents, decrees, and stationary (fig. 9). All are comparable in their obedience to the principle of hieroglyphic visual writing.

FIGURE 7. Janinet, after Moitte, *Liberty*, circa 1793, engraving, Paris, Bibliothèque Nationale, Cabinet des Estampes, Collection De Vinck, No. 6050. Reproduced by permission.

In the realm of painting, an extreme example of such visual writing stands out: Jean-Baptiste Regnault's *Liberty or Death* (fig. 4). It is especially interesting for structural simplifications that contrast radically to the painter's 1792 *Allegory on the*

LA FRANCE RÉPUBLICAINE.

Ouvrant son Sein à tous les Français.

FIGURE 8. Clément, after Boizot, *Republican France Offering Her Breasts to all the French*, circa 1794, engraving, Paris, Bibliothèque Nationale, Cabinet des Estampes, Collection De Vinck, No. 6074. Reproduced by permission.

Declaration of the Rights of Man (fig. 10). With some two dozen figures, the earlier painting is typical of the way so many Revolutionary allegories grafted new political content to traditional forms. Completed at the end of 1793, the large version of

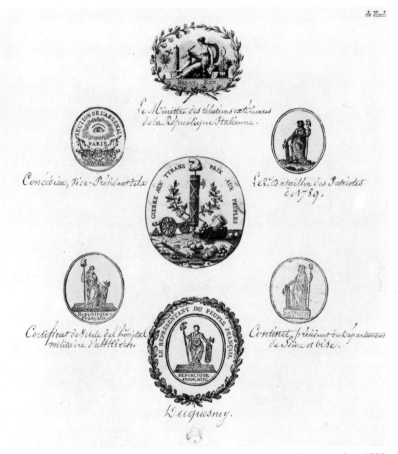

FIGURE 9. Group of Seven Vignettes from Revolutionary Stationary, circa 1793, engravings, Paris, Bibliothèque Nationale, Cabinet des Estampes, Collection De Vinck, No. 4831. Reproduced by permission.

the *Liberty or Death* was offered by the artist to the Nation. Now lost, it is documented at the Hall of the Council of Five-Hundred from 1799 to 1805.[45] First shown during the Thermidorian Reaction, the painting was attacked politically as "suitable for flattering Robespierre and his agents."[46] It is a visual translation of the motto of the Constitution of the Year III: "Liberty, Equality, Fraternity, or Death." Though its origins are in the less intimidating "Live Free or Die," Regnault's interpretation makes this our most obvious example of Revolutionary art as interpellation.[47]

FIGURE 10. Regnault, *Allegory on the Declaration of the Rights of Man*, 1790, oil on canvas, Versailles, Musée Lambin. Reproduced by permission.

The *Liberty or Death* in a sense inverts the relationship between realism and writing that we find in the *Marat*. The conflict between illusionistic sky, clouds, earthly orb, and the canvas' role as support for allegorical writing, is resolved through a kind of hyper-realism. The interpellative character of the Regnault derives from the painter's ability to give Revolutionary symbols "actual presence"—to give them a life beyond the allegorical. In this form of realism, painted forms are perceived not only as allegories but as realistic images. The hieroglyph becomes performative by appearing to be part of physical reality. The figures offering their frightening choice gaze relentlessly outward towards the viewer, insisting on contact with the present world. The viewer is shaped by that gaze. The genie of France, identified by his tricolor wings, seems to lean into the space in front of the picture. The woman, who can be read interchangeably as The Republic, France, or Liberty, holds up the Revolutionary bonnet, a Jacobin adaptation of the cap worn by Phrygians as a sign of freedom from slavery. In her other hand, the figure holds a mason's level for Equality. (Regnault was a Freemason.) Against the bright sky, its triangular form may allude to another Masonic adaptation from Egypt, the vigilant eye and the pyramid. At her feet lie the sheaf of fasces, a common symbol for Fraternity which also alludes to the Roman ideal of collective authority. The snake biting its tail on the throne's side signifies eternity, an idea less pleasantly introduced by the figure of Death.[48]

As a representation of Revolution, this painting centers on abstract concepts, which are impersonally configured with stock symbols. Whereas the *Marat* conceives the Revolution as an individual enactment of ideas, the *Liberty or Death* presents ideas themselves as living and compelling—even coercive. The performative power of the *Marat* is linked to David's personal presence and activities. Regnault's signature merely records an act of civic duty. Power of representation is implicitly attributed to some abstract source within the picture—Revolutionary power—which Regnault characterizes as impersonal and from which he dissociates himself. His picture reads as that power's self-representation. While thus at opposite poles, both the *Marat* and the *Liberty or Death* nevertheless share the confrontational psychology and structural emblematicity I have linked to the paradigm of visual writing. Produced for the state, the Regnault takes life and legibility from a widely disseminated official

FIGURE 11. David, *The French Republic Triumphing over Monarchy*, Project for Curtain for the Opéra, 1794, Drawing, Paris, Musée Carnavelet. Reproduced by permission.

repertory of hieroglyphs. France is present both internally as symbol and externally as audience giving meaning to its symbolic code. It is both interpellator and the subject of interpellation. Just as France is itself divided by its two choices, the painting thus posits an internal division in its representation of France. Its rigor, though clearly addressed to a divided France, serves only to heighten that division rather than to overcome it.

Besides temporary works he designed for festivals, David's project for the curtain of the Opera (fig. 11) may be the closest thing he did to the kind of allegory exemplified in the Regnault and in Revolutionary prints. It was to coincide with the performance of a "sans-culotide [sic] dramatique" written by Gabriel Bouquier, another artist-député with whom David had collaborated. Presented in five acts "in verse mixed with declamations," the scenario was directly inspired by David's Festival of Unity and Indivisibility of the Republic. Yet in addition to its connection to the festivals or to funerary processions he organized, the curtain's image of the Republic on a triumphal chariot maintained contact with reality by mixing contemporary heroes with those of antiquity.[49] Conceptually, it is half-way between the *Marat* and the *Liberty or Death*.

Lacking an urgent confrontational presence, David's opera curtain remained a traditional exercise, whereas the *Liberty or Death* shocked its audience, which was free after Thermidor to attack its strangeness. We discover terms of horror, not unlike those evoked by the *Marat*. In the introduction to a series of letters on the Salon of 1795, one critic implied a specific character to the art of the period of the Terror by calling "bizarre" the results of trying to make a revolution in the arts as well as in politics.[50] A writer with the aristocratic *particule* said that the *Liberty or Death*'s red bonnet reminded him of "bloody entrails;" another complained that Regnault should have been able to paint liberty without death ("sans nous donner la mort").[51] Both comments, though overtly political, testify to the image's performative power. Other observers concentrated on pictorial matters. The painting was attacked for a "symmetrical disposition" and for being poorly unified ("décousu"), for lack of transition between figures.[52] In other words, it was attacked for precisely those elements of emblematicity and disjunctiveness that differentiate it from Regnault's earlier allegory.

I argued earlier that the *Marat* represents the individual, as its hero, as its creator, and as its audience. Inducing the act of

FIGURE 12. Anonymous, *Declaration of the Rights of Man, with large figure of the French Republic*, August 1793, engraving, Paris, Bibliothèque Nationale, Cabinet des Estampes, Collection De Vinck, No. 4231. Reproduced by permission.

mourning, an essentially private act, the painting detaches its viewer from his or her social context to appeal directly to emotions. Yet publicly expressed, such mourning became a basis for a new and Revolutionary bonding, establishing a new, fraternal basis for society. The Regnault operates similarly to isolate its viewer, yet differently, to bond him to abstract concepts rather than through socialization. The painting's figures are perceived—as words are—as separable entities. Not only are they solitary symbols floating in the ether of a utopian tabula rasa,

INTÉRIEUR D'UN COMITÉ RÉVOLUTIONNAIRE SOUS LE RÉGIME DE LA TERREUR
Années 1793 et 1794, ou Années 2ᵉ et 3ᵉ de la République.

FIGURE 13. Berthauld, after Fragonard, fils, *The Interior of a Revolutionary Committee During the Terror*, circa June 1794, engraving, Paris, Bibliothèque Nationale, Cabinet des Estampes, Collection De Vinck, No. 6483. Reproduced by permission.

they are mutually exclusive terms in a semantic structure. The painting suppresses the theme of collective action pre-eminent in so many illustrations of Revolutionary events. In contrast to the experience of theater, it posits an audience of solitary individuals molded by ideas rather than by experience. Its structure is more like a mise-en-page than a mise-en-scène. Conventional discourse might well characterize this interpellation as "bizarre." Yet that is the process of Revolution: stripping individuals of connections with one social order to create a new solidarity based solely on ideas—deconstitution/reconstitution.

Contemporary engravings demonstrate the extent to which Revolutionary symbolism was pervasive. A richly ornamented Declaration of the Rights of Man contains many of the features we have seen and adds some others (fig. 12). An engraving showing a Revolutionary committee room during the Terror shows how objects such as swords, bonnets, busts of heroes, and so on were standard paraphernalia (fig. 13). There is no reason to

FIGURE 14. Juillet, after Ranson, *Tableau civique with Republican Guards*, 1794, colored engraving, Paris, Bibliothèque Nationale, Cabinet des Estampes, Collection De Vinck, No. 6126. Reproduced by permission.

suppose that for opponents of the Revolution such displays were much less distasteful than are the symbols of the Nazi party for most of us today. My point, which is not to compare Jacobinism with Fascism politically, is that such an extensive apparatus inevitably engenders a psychology of coercion and surveillance. The layout of a Tableau Civique bordered by Republican Guards alludes directly to that situation (fig. 14). By a decree of March 29, 1793, which followed by eight days the establishment of Committees of Revolutionary Surveillance, the Convention required landlords to post tenants' names outside each house. While such symbols call for rational decoding, similar to the viewing of narrative art, in a context of pervasive familiarity they perform their effect immediately and unconsciously upon the emotions. Reflecting a dialectic of order and disorder, representations of Revolution inevitably imply features contradictory to their own ideals. For the process of Revolution begins with contradiction.

Over time, the *Marat* has come to seem compelling rather than coercive, humanistic rather than totalitarian, unlike the divisive *Liberty or Death*. Its connections to political factions and violence forgotten, and in the absence of its author's rhetoric, the *Marat* survives with elements of continuity and order rather than the opposite. It becomes the kind of image a democratic state can take for itself, once its political references—its evidence of disorder—"disappear behind a moral allegory," as Antoine Schnapper writes.[53] Though Regnault was the more politically moderate artist, David, whose ultimate discourse is of self-realization rather than coercion, instinctively produced the more politically malleable work. The flat, abstract and utopian *Liberty or Death*, despite obvious elements of both classicism and modernity, still seems "bizarre." Its failure to achieve normative status is linked to a fundamentally divided structure that makes its connections to factional reality inescapable. Now buried in a basement somewhere, it defies assimilation to the myth of the Revolution as an orderly stage in the development of democratic society.

NOTES

1. See François Furet, *Interpreting the French Revolution* (Cambridge, 1981), and Lynn Hunt, *Politics, Culture, and Class in the French Revolution* (Berkeley, 1984).

2. See Renaud Barral, "Les Jacobins penseurs de leur propre Révolution," in *Philosophies de la Révolution française: représentations et interprétations* (Paris, 1984), 17-31, and Jean-Marie Goulemot, "Le mot *Révolution* et la formation du concept de *révolution politique* (fin XVIIe siècle)," *Annales historiques de la Révolution française* 197 (1967): 417-444.

3. J.L. Austin, *How to do Things with Words* (Cambridge, Mass., 1962).

4. Ibid., 5.

5. Ibid., 60-61.

6. See William Olander, "The Concours de l'an II," *The Consortium on Revolutionary Europe, Proceedings* (1980): 2:19-27.

7. This is the theme of Linda Nochlin, "The Realist Criminal and the Abstract Law," in Richard Hertz, ed., *Theories of Contemporary Art* (Englewood Cliffs N.J., 1985), 25-48.

8. Robert L. Herbert, *David, Voltaire, 'Brutus,' and the French Revolution: An Essay in Art and Politics* (London and New York, 1972).

9. See my "Painting and Politics, II: J.-L. David's Patriotism, or the Conspiracy of Gracchus Bebeuf and the Legacy of Topino-Lebrun," *Art Bulletin* 58 (1976): 547-568.

10. On the centrality of the Terror to the Revolution and recent attempts to "débarrasser notre démocratie de l'origine révolutionnaire," see Jean-Michel Besnier, "La Révolution contre la Démocratie? Les analyses de la Terreur et leurs implications, ou Que faire de Robespierre?" *Revue de l'Institut catholique*, no. 13 (Jan.-Mar. 1985): 53-79.

11. Louis Marin, *Le Portrait du roi* (Paris, 1981), and "Le Corps glorieux du Roi et son portrait," in *La Parole mangée et autres essais théologico-politiques* (Paris, 1986), 195-225.

12. Mona Ozouf, *La Fête révolutionnaire, 1789-1799* (Paris, 1976), 16.

13. *Convention nationale. Rapport et décret sur la fête de la réunion républicaine du 10 août, présentés au nom du Comité d'instruction publique (le 11 juillet 1793) par David* (Paris, n.d.).

14. See Ozouf, *La Fête révolutionnaire*, "La fête et l'espace," 149-187, and "Rien ne va sans dire," 253-259.

15. For the concept that "ideology interpellates individuals as subjects," see Louis Althusser, "Ideology and Ideological State Apparatuses," in *Lenin and Philosophy and Other Essays*, trans, Ben Brewster (London, 1971), 121-173, esp. 160-165.

16. See Albert Boime, "Marmontel's *Bélisaire* and the Pre-Revolutionary Progressivism of David," *Art History* 3 (March 1980): 81-101; Thomas Crow, "The Oath of the Horatii in 1785: Painting and Pre-Revolutionary Radicalism in France," *Art History* 1 (December 1978): 424-471; and Herbert, *Brutus.*

17. On the Revolutionary theory of art, see James A. Leith, *The Idea of Art as Propaganda in France, 1750-1799* (Toronto, 1965), and Diane Kelder, *Aspects of "Official" Painting and Philosophic Art, 1789-1799* (New York, 1976).

18. There is no better documented account of these activities than David Dowd, *Pageant-Master of the Republic: Jacques-Louis David and the French Revolution* (Lincoln, Neb., 1948).

19. Two recent works will provide access to the extensive bibliographies on this painting. Jean-Claude Bonnet, ed., *La Mort de Marat* (Paris, 1986), contains articles on the historical phenomenon of Marat's death, with several, cited further on, that touch on the painting. Jörg Traeger, *Der Tod des Marat* (Munich, 1986), is as complete a monograph as has yet been published.

20. "Il est effectivement difficile d'en soutenir longtemps la vue [of the painting], tant l'effet en est terrible." *Exposition dans la cour du Louvre des tableaux de Lepeletier et de Marat*, 16 October 1793, in Bibliothèque Nationale, Estampes, Collection Deloynes, LIV, No. 1584.

21. Daniel and Guy Wildenstein, *Documents complémentaires au catalogue de l'oeuvre de Louis David* (Paris, [1973]), No. 360.

22. Etienne-Jean Delécluze, *David, son école et son temps* (Paris, 1855), 153.

23. Two recent articles published side by side in German relate this duality to contemporary events: Klaus Herding, "David's 'Marat' als *dernier appel à l'unité révolutionnaire*," and Willibald Sauerländer, "David's 'Marat à son dernier soupir' oder Malerei und Terreur," in Werner Hofmann and Martin Warnke, eds., *Kunst um 1800, Idea: Jahrbuch der Hamburger Kunsthalle* 2 (1983): 89-112 and 49-88. The phrase "reportage and epitaph" is from the latter (70), though the idea of the painting's essential duality was most eloquently expressed by Charles Baudelaire, "Le Musée classique du Bazar Bonne-Nouvelle" (1846), in Henri

Lemaître, ed., *Curiosités esthétiques, l'art romantique et autres oeuvres critiques* (Paris, 1962), 89. For a historiographical approach to the Baudelairian duality: Jean-Rémy Mantion, "Enveloppes à Marat David," in *La Mort de Marat*, 203-232.

24. Chantal Thomas, ("Portraits de Charlotte Corday," in *La Mort de Marat*, 271-286) notes that Charlotte Corday's absence from David's picture depersonalizes Marat's death to the advantage of its use as a representation of Revolution (276).

25. Gérard Walter, *Marat* (Paris, 1953), cited by Sauerländer, 71.

26. The point about stylelessness has been made by Norman Bryson, *Word and Image: French Painting of the Ancien Régime* (Cambridge, 1981), 245-246, though with a different purpose.

27. In offering the painting to the Convention, David suggests this was a deliberate effect: "... que ses [Marat's] ennemis pâlissent encore en voyant ses traits défigurés ... " *Discours prononcé à la Convention nationale par David ... en lui offrant le tableau représentant Marat assassiné* (Séance du 25 brumaire l'an II de la République française [Paris, n.d.]; the full text is cited below, note 36). An excellent and heretofore essential account of official and press reports of Marat's death stresses the same duality. See Jacques Gilhaumou, "La Mort de Marat à Paris (13 juillet-16 juillet 1793)," in *La Mort de Marat*, 39-80.

28. Denials of Marat's death and efforts to make him relive are recounted in Ibid. 61-78.

29. Herding, "David's 'Marat,'" 105, sees the religious side of the painting as addressed to the people and the ancient hero side to the Convention.

30. Herbert, *Brutus*, 101, gives three sources: *Section du Muséum; Ordre de la marche; Pompe funèbre pour l'inauguration des bustes de Marat et de Lepeletier*, October 16, 1793; *Exposition dans la cour du Louvre des tableaux de Lepeletier et de Marat*, October 16, 1793; and Alexandre Lenoir, "David, Souvenirs historiques," *Journal de l'Institut historique* 3 (August 2, 1835): 1-13.

31. Frank Paul Bowman, "Le 'Sacré-Coeur' de Marat" (1793), in Jean Ehrard and Paul Viallaneix, eds., *Les Fêtes de la Révolution. Actes du Colloque de Clermont-Ferrand (juin 1974)* (Paris, 1977), 155-179.

32. On the emblematic character of representations of Marat see Lise Andries, "Les Estampes de Marat sous la Révolution: Une Emblématique," in *La Mort de Marat*, 187-201.

33. *Discours*, 25 brumaire l'an II.

34. The painting of Lepeletier contains writing that is closer than anything in the *Marat* to a descriptive legend. The sword hanging by a thread over Lepeletier's body pierces a parchment inscribed with the words: "Je vote la mort du tyran." The device recalls the I.N.R.I. at the top of Christ's cross or banderoles often found in Medieval and early Renaissance religious painting. It also contained a dedicatory signature, as in the *Marat*, and like the *Marat* the painting's composition recalled the public funeral ceremony David had organized, with its display of Lepeletier's body on a hero's neo-antique deathbed. (For a history of the painting and a description, see Maurice Tourneux, "Notes pour servir à l'histoire d'un chef-d'oeuvre inconnu: Le Peletier sur son lit de mort, par David," in *Nouvelles Archives de l'art francais*, 3e série, 5 (1889): 52-59.) The most popular legend accompanying the image of the dead Marat was: "N'ayant pu le corrompre, ils l'ont assassiné." (See Andries, "Les Estampes de Marat," in *La Mort de Marat*, 197).

35. "L'expression de l'horreur de ces deux portraits est répandue tant dans leur ensemble que dans les détails, ce qui prouve que la touche mâle et savante de l'artiste n'aurait pas seule suffi et qu'il fallait encore cet ardent amour pour la

patrie dont il est enflammé." *Exposition dans la cour du Louvre.* These words may be compared to those of the artist himself: "Le peuple redemandait son ami, sa voix désolée se faisait entendre, il provoquait mon art, il voulait revoir les traits de son ami fidèle: David! saisis tes pinceaux, s'écria-t-il, venge notre ami, venge Marat; que ses ennemis vaincus pâlissent encore en voyant ses trait défigurés, réduis-les à envier le sort de celui que, n'ayant pu le corrompre, ils on eu la lâcheté de faire assassiner. J'ai entendu la voix de peuple, j'ai obéi." *Discours,* 25 brumaire l'an II.

36. Philippe Bordes, *'Le Serment du Jeu de Paume' de Jacques-Louis David: le peintre, son milieu et son temps, de 1789 à 1792* (Paris, 1983), places the painting within the traditions of contemporary history painting. On that subject, see William Olander, *Pour transmettre la postérité: French Painting and Revolution, 1774-1795* (Ann Arbor, 1984).

37. On the Revolutionary preoccupation with language, see Hunt, *Politics, Culture, and Class,* 19-51, "The Rhetoric of Revolution."

38. Ferdinand Brunot, *Histoire de la langue française, des origines à nos jours, IX: La Révolution et l'Empire* (Paris, 1967), p. 3.

39. *Révolutions de Paris,* IX, September 9, 1789, 25-26. Cited by Stanley J. Idzerda, "Iconoclasm during the French Revolution," *American Historical Review* 60 (1954): 16.

40. "Il n'y a rien de plus contraire aux intérêts du peuple et de l'égalité que d'être difficile sur le langage." Cited in Denis Roche, *"La Liberté ou la mort: réfléchissez et choisissez,"* 1789 (Collection, "Les Murs ont la parole") (Paris, 1969), 6.

41. Idzerda, "Iconoclasm," 13-26.

42. "Que la parole soit désormais notre seul instrument." Cited by Ozouf, *La Fête révolutionnaire,* 258.

43. See Judith Schlanger, "Le Peuple au front gravé," in Ehrard and Villaneix, eds., *Les Fêtes de la Révolution,* 387-395. Schlanger writes in more general terms (389): "Le verbal est alors globalement le socle de la vision et en quelque sorte son matériau et sa finalité." Thus, referring to the statue project (388), allegory "n'arrive à la plénitude que si elle n'est pas muette."

44. For illustrations, see Jean-Paul Bouillon, Monique Mosser and Daniel Rabreau, *Les Fêtes de la Révolution,* exh. cat., Musée Bargoin (Clermont-Ferrand, 1974).

45. See *French Painting 1774-1830: The Age of Revolution,* No. 150. The painting was done in fulfillment of an encouragement prize that allowed Regnault free choice of subject. When the painting was offered to the Convention in 1794, with the suggestion that it decorate the Salle des Séances (where the *Marat* and the *Lepeletier* already hung), the artist was acclaimed, but the painting was sent to be examined by the Jury des Arts. ("Offrande du tableau de Regnault à la Convention," Bibliothèque Nationale, Estampes, Collection Deloynes, XVIII, No. 479.)

46. Rob..., *Exposition publique... dans le Salon du Louvre, au mois de septembre, année 1795,* Paris, Bibliothéque Nationale, Estampes, Collection Deloynes, XVIII, No. 469.

47. On the origins of the motto, see Raoul Bonnet, "La Liberté ou la Mort," *La Révolution française* (1923): 19-22. It cannot be dismissed as innocuous. For example, Duhamel and Perrotin, with the approval of Collot d'Herbois and Fouché added "réfléchissez et choisissez" to the motto in their instructions of 26

Brumaire, Year II (November 16, 1793) to the constitutional authorities of the Rhêne and Loire departments. (See the explanation in Roche, *La Liberté*, title page.)

48. For symbols of the Republic, see Jules Renouvier, *Histoire de l'art pendant la Révolution* (Paris, 1863), 391-415; Maurice Agulhon, *Marianne into Battle: Republican Imagery and Symbolism in France, 1789-1880*, tr. Janet Lloyd (Cambridge, 1981), 15-22; and Jennifer Harris, "The Red Cap of Liberty: A Study of Dress Worn by French Revolutionary Partisans, 1789-94," *Eighteenth Century Studies* 14 (Spring 1981): 283-312.

49. Gabriel Bouquier and P.L. Moline, *La Réunion du dix août, ou l'Inauguration de la République française*, sanculotide dramatique en 5 actes et en vers mêlé de déclamations, chants, danses et évolutions militaires, Paris, Year II. See Antoine Schnapper, *David, témoin de son temps* (Paris, 1980): 143-146, and *La Révolution française, Le Premier Empire: Dessins du Musée Carnavalet* (Paris, 1983), no. 23.

50. "Lettres de Polyscope sur les ouvrages de peinture, sculpture, etc. exposés dans le grand Salon du Muséum, 1795," First letter, Deloynes, No. 471.

51. J.H. de la Ser, *Examen critique de plus beaux ouvrages exposés au Salon du Louvre de cette année 1795*, Paris, l'an IV, 6, and *Critique sur les tableaux exposés au Salon, l'an 4e*, Collection Deloynes, XVIII, no. 476.

52. Rob . . . , "Réflexions sur l'exposition des Tableaux, sculptures, etc. de l'an 4e 1795, . . . extrait du *Mercure de France*," Deloynes, No. 470, and "Lettres de Polyscope," Second letter, Deloynes, No. 472.

53. Schnapper, *David*, 158.

THE OPENING OF THE DEPTHS

Peter Brooks

In a dusty corner of the Musée Carnavalet in Paris, one can find the ladders, constructed from bedsheets and firewood, that purportedly were used by Henri Masers de Latude in his escape from the Bastille in 1756. Latude spent little time at liberty; he was apprehended, returned to the Bastille, then transferred to other prisons—Vincennes, Charenton, Bicêtre—and finally released in 1784 after a total of thirty-five years in confinement for having insulted Madame de Pompadour. He became celebrated through his Memoirs, the first version of them, in 1787, apparently apocryphal, a later authorized version prepared by the lawyer Thiery. When the Bastille was stormed on July 14, 1789, Latude's ladders, and various other tools manufactured for his ingenious escape, were found in the *greffe* of the prison. They were put on public display in 1834, in the foyer of the Théâre de la Gaîté, for the opening of Guilbert de Pixerécourt's "mélodrame historique," *Latude, ou trente-cinq ans de captivité*. This was the last great success of the playwright known as the "Corneille of the Boulevards," and the play he chose to close the fourth and final volume of his *Théâtre choisi*. It sums up not only dominant themes and situations in Pixerécourt's vast melodramatic production, but as well an obsessive imaginative focus of melodrama from the moment of its creation, during the Revolution. Pixerécourt's play is about the nightmare of captivity, life constrained in the dungeon, unable to assert its rights, unable to make heard its claim to innocence. Latude's rightful name is even changed in the prison registers, to ensure that he will never be able to nominate himself as what he is, the victim of arbitrary tyranny. His companion in imprisonment and confederate in his ill-starred escape, Dalègre, finally goes mad from the deprivations of captivity, and by the end hallucinates himself in the role of jailer and torturer rather than victim. The opening of the prison, performed in the last act of the play by the enlightened minister Malesherbes, reveals a sorry spectacle, the underside of the Age of Reason.

From July 14, 1789, onwards, the Bastille will be taken and opened up and torn down hundreds of times in the theatres of

Paris, in vaudevilles and melodramas using various story lines to reach this glorious moment. The prison and the aspiration for liberation become dominant themes in the French and European imagination, as Victor Brombert has so well shown.[1] From those popular plays entitled *La Prise de la Bastille* or some slight variant thereof to the melodramas of the Empire and the Restoration—*Le Château des Appenins, Les Mines de Pologne, La Forteresse du Danube*—to the memoirs of Silvio Pellico and Alexandre Andryane, to the novels of Stendhal and Hugo, to Beethoven's *Fidelio* and the operas of Verdi, the prison is everywhere, the act of liberation a salutation to a new era in which the rights of man will be a fundamental guarantee, the freedom to dispose of one's own mind and body an irreducible test of civilization.

But what interests me here is less the aspiration to liberty than what one finds when the liberators open the prisons, what lies concealed in the depths and comes to light with the gesture of liberation. Here, I think, one encounters something less clearly progressive and beneficent than the simple setting free of prisoners. The act of opening up releases a certain repressed which reason has ignored. It is here that the structure of fortress and prison, with moats, drawbridges, towers and, especially, layer upon layer of subterranean *cachots* and *oubliettes*, comes to resemble a Freudian conceptualization of the mind as a spatialized construct of the conscious, the preconscious, and the unconscious, and the uncovering of repressed material as an archeological excavation into ever more deeply buried strata of psychic life.[2] Some of the best representations of this structure come in those Revolutionary dramas sometimes labeled as *théâtre monacal*: dramas of forced religious vocations and diabolical abbots and abbesses which always include subterranean crypts and *in pace* where the virtuous are confined and tortured until release arrives.[3] While this Gothic situation can be found in novels and plays that predate the Revolution—for the Revolution was culturally as well as politically prepared, anticipated in the realm of *l'imaginaire* as well as in those of *le politique* and *le social*—the storming of the Bastille and then the attacks on the clergy and on monasticism give it a new vigor and popularity during the Revolution, in plays such as *Les Rigueurs du cloître*, by Fiévée (1790), *Le Couvant, ou les voeux forcés* (1790), by Olympe de Gouges, *Les Victîmes cloîtrées* (1791), by Boutet de Monvel, *Fénelon, ou les religieuses de Cambrai* (1793), by Marie-Joseph Chénier, *Julie, ou la Religieuse de Nismes* (1796), by

Charles Pougens, among many others. Particularly following the liberation of the theatres on January 13, 1791, there was full flowering of melodramatic treatments of the theme.

I want to dwell for just a moment on Boutet de Monvel's *Les Victîmes cloîtrées*, which has often been called the first melodrama (though the label had not yet come into use), presented to the acclamations of the audience by the Comédiens-Français on March 29, 1791. In this play, monastic, political, and erotic intrigue converge to the point where they are indistinguishable. The evil Père Laurent cloisters the innocent Eugénie against her will—ostensibly to please the aristocrat Madame de Saint-Alban, who wants to prevent her mésalliance with the merchant Dorval—but really in order to pursue his own libidinous designs on her; while Madame de Saint-Alban's brother, the virtuous Francheville, has been elected mayor by *his concitoyens*, and combats Dorval's desperate resolution to cloister himself (abetted by Père Laurent, who wants Dorval's fortune) through arguments that a young man should put his talents at the service of *la patrie*. To no avail. By the fourth act, both Eugénie and Dorval have been consigned to the deepest *in pace* cells of the convent and the monastery, respectively, which, it so happens, are built side by side, and share a common wall. So that the decor of the fourth and final act shows two prison cells, one stage left, the other stage right, the one containing Eugénie, the other Dorval, each of whom pursues a soliloquy of despair. But before Père Laurent comes to pursue his designs on Eugénie, Dorval discovers a tunnel from the one cell to the other, nearly completed by a predecessor prisoner who spent twenty years at labor on it before expiring. To the cry of "Liberté! liberté! soutiens-moi!" Dorval completes the tunnel, and comes through to Eugénie's cell. Noises are heard on the stairs leading down to the cells. Eugénie and Dorval prepare to die fighting, when the door opens to reveal the party of the virtuous, escorted by the municipal police and led by Francheville draped in his mayoral *tricolore* sash, who have overcome Père Laurent and his henchmen and come to free the victims. Francheville sums up: "O mes concitoyens! vous voyez les bienfaits de la loi. . . . And a virtuous monk, Père Louis, has the curtain line, announcing that he will leave the monastery: "je vais briser les chaînes que la violence m'imposa si longtemps."

The chains of violent constraint are broken, the victims of tyrannical oppression are liberated from the depths, republicanism triumphs. Yet there remains the image of that fourth-act setting, the deepest dungeon, where prisoners are deprived of justice and of their very identity, and where the female victim is subject to the erotic will of her persecutor. One may be reminded of Robert-Fleury's famous painting of Pinel ordering the chains taken off the madwomen of the Salpêtrière when he assumed its direction in 1795: along with the gesture of liberation, we remain forcibly impressed by the anguished faces and twisted bodies of the madwomen. If the Revolution constituted a solar myth, as Jean Starobinski puts it, the light of reason that it shed kept illuminating situations of unreason, shadows of the human heart and mind that could not be so simply dispersed.[4]

Among the members of the audience at *Les Victîmes cloîtrées* was a young Englishman, Matthew Gregory Lewis, who was so impressed by Monvel's work that he translated and adapted it as *Venoni, or the Novice of St. Mark's*, which was staged at Drury Lane in 1808. As the title implies, Lewis has changed the place of the drama—to Sicily—and the identity of some of the characters, especially Francheville, "who in the original," he notes, "was a Republican Mayor, whose sentiments and conduct were by no means adapted to the present times or to the British taste."[5] Lewis goes on, in his preface, to concede that while his first two acts were well-received at the first performance, "the last was by no means equally successful, and the concluding scene operated so strongly on the risible muscles of the audience, as to make it evident to me on the third night, that unless I could invent an entirely new last act, the piece must be given up altogether." So he substituted a new third act, and the play continued a successful run—interrupted only by the burning down of Drury Lane Theatre. Lewis maintains that the original last act was nonetheless preferable. Yet it could not work, I think, because once stripped of its political symbolism, the scene of liberation lost much of its power. Surely there were no "risible muscles" at work at the Théâtre de la Nation in 1791: the stakes of the opening of the depths were clear.

I mention Lewis's drama because between seeing *Les Victîmes cloîtrées* and producing *Venoni*, Lewis wrote his masterwork, *The Monk* (published in 1795 or 1796), a novel that was clearly inspired by Monvel's play and which, despite the nationality of its author and its transposition of events to other times and places, may legitimately, if somewhat perversely, be considered the greatest novel to come out of the French Revolution. And it was in fact a work that at once returned to France, in the form of numerous translations, imitations and, especially, theatrical adaptations, including one by Pixerécourt himself.[6] *The Monk* takes as its setting Spain, at an unidentified date but one at which the Inquisition appears to reign supreme. Through his masterful evocation of the penetrating omnipresence of the Inquisition, Lewis creates a powerful image of any regime of unreason and arbitrary tyranny. And in the churches, monasteries and, especially, the Convent of St. Clare that stand at the center of his novel, he creates the essential spaces of claustration, and within them the horrible monsters engendered by the sleep of reason and freedom.

I won't attempt to rehearse the complex plot of *The Monk*, which turns on the gradual conversion of Ambrosio, the holy abbot of the Capuchins, into a lustful monster who enters into pacts with the infernal powers in order to pursue his erotic needs. Ambrosio is first seduced by the novice Rosario, who turns out to be not a young man but a woman in disguise, Matilda, who has in fact served as the model for the icon of the Madonna that Ambrosio worships. So that the very vehicle of his sublimation of profane love in love divine becomes the instrument of the return of the repressed: the ambiguous figure of Rosario/Matilda unleashes the nether side of a passion Ambrosio thought to be wholly spiritual. Once she has seduced Ambrosio, Matilda initiates him into the practice of diabolical conjurations in order to perpetrate the seduction of the beautiful and virginal Antonia, whose mother he is forced to kill along the way, while he has Antonia drugged and removed to the deepest cell of the sepulchre of St. Clare, the better to practice upon her virtue. Meanwhile— in the novel's even wilder subplot—the pregnant Agnes has been separated from her lover, Don Raymond, and also entombed living in the underground sepulchre of St. Clare, in a punishment meted out by the hypocritical Domina of the convent, where she will have her baby amidst skeletons and decaying corpses. Thus the climax of all the tales of passion in *The Monk* will have to be played out in the deepest dungeons of the convent, accessible only through a hidden door concealed under the base of the statue of St. Clare, and by way of Piranesi-like staircases into the subterranean gloom. At the same time, the disappearance of Agnes and other young women has become public knowledge, and the populace rises in revolt against the Domina and the convent, murdering the one, setting fire to the other.

This, in brief, is the context in which both Don Lorenzo, brother of Agnes and enamored of Antonia, and Ambrosio go into the depths in the final chapters of the novel. First Lorenzo: he discovers a door into the sepulchre from the cemetery, and hears the sound of footsteps leading deep into "the labyrinth of passages."[7] Leaving behind daylight and rationality, Lorenzo finds himself "impelled by a movement secret and unaccountable" into the sepulchre, until he undercovers the grate hidden under the statue of St. Clare, which, raised, shows the entrance to the true underworld: "A deep abyss now presented itself before them, whose thick obscurity the eye strove in vain to pierce" (353). The fearful nuns gathered at the statue refuse to accompany him in his descent. "Alone therefore, and in darkness, he prepared to pursue his design . . . " (354). Down, down into the "gulph" he descends, as by compulsion, until finally in a "loathesome abode" he finds his beloved Agnes, clutching a bundle that turns out to be the corpse of her baby.

Agnes will fill in the full narrative of her prison sojourn momentarily, a story of lizards, toads, worms, and the excruciating agony of the slow death of the child. Meanwhile, we return to another part of the sepulchre, where the drugged Antonia has been confined, and Ambrosio prepares to further his designs on her: "By the side of three putrid half-corrupted bodies lay the sleeping beauty" (363). Ambrosio's words of seduction suggest the identity of the dungeon with the deepest recess of forbidden desire: "This sepulchre seems to me Love's bower. This gloom is the friendly night of Mystery, which he spreads over our delights! Such do I think it, and such must my Antonia. Yes, my sweet girl! yes! Your veins shall flow with the fire which circles in mine, and my transports shall be doubled by your sharing them!" (366). But she resists such seductions, and he is reduced to raping her. Immediately thereafter, he is seized by "disgust" (which may be the most frequently-repeated word in the novel) at his despoiling of innocence. But he cannot release her to tell her tale. The only solution he can propose is a life in the sepulchre: "Wretched girl, you must stay here with me! Here amidst these lonely tombs, these images of death, these rotting, loathesome, corrupted bodies! Here shall you stay, and witness my sufferings; witness what it is to be in the horrors of despondency, and breathe the last groan in blasphemy and curses!" (369). When Antonia attempts to flee, he finally murders her.

To heighten further this frenetic drama it turns out that, all unbeknownst to the actors, Ambrosio and Antonia are brother and sister, thus the rape also an incest, the murder a fratricide, and the killing of Antonia's mother a matricide. It is in the logic of Ambrosio's towering sexual passion, once it has broken through the layers of denial and repression, that it should violate all the ultimate taboos. If the depths represent the effects of repression, pushing eros down into the deepest recess, once one penetrates into those depths one finds sexuality gone berserk, playing out scenarios of an unconscious that does not recognize contradiction. Incest in particular, as the taboo demarcating culture from nature and thus founding society, will have a long history in Romantic texts, as a temptation barely escaped, and often will be associated with the claustral space: think, for instance, of Chateaubriand's *René*, where Amélie's confession of her incestuous desire for her brother comes at the moment she is stretched out on a gravestone, during the *office des morts* that prepares her taking of the veil. The convent, the dungeon, the sepulchre are where the most intense and interdicted passions— interdicted because intense, intense because interdicted—come to be confined, and when one penetrates into the place of confinement, one finds the enactment of desires that reason and the daylight self do not avow.

This is the image that *The Monk* most forcefully impresses upon us: that in opening the depths, we not only perform an act of beneficent liberation, we also discover something much more troubling, something that political versions of liberation are not adequate to account for or deal with—an image already implicit in *Les Victîmes cloîtrées*. Claustration is itself the space of a psychic liberation, but of forces that political liberation needs to repress. Consider, in a final reflection on *The Monk*, Ambrosio's trial before the Inquisition, in the last chapter. The narrator tells us: "In these trials neither the accusation is mentioned, nor the name of the accuser. The prisoners are only asked, whether they will confess. If they reply, that, having no crime, they can make no confession, they are put to the torture without delay" (403). Such a procedure appears in some ways as the very opposite of the Revolutionary tribunal, where denunciations are specific and often made in person. It is, one might say, the procedure appropriate for a world in which everyone is guilty, of unspecified crimes which are in the nature of man himself. It

gives an image of guilt appropriate to post-Freudian man, living
in the knowledge that psychic recesses harbor a freight of
repressed desires normally excluded from consciousness.

The person who best understood the complicity of the claustral
space with the release of repressed desire—indeed their mutual
interdependence—was, of course, the Marquis de Sade, whose
whole *oeuvre* narrates and dramatizes this connection. And in the
work in which he brings his most sustained analytic attention to
the Revolution—the tract "Français encore un effort si vous
voulez être républicains," inserted into *La Philosophie dans le
boudoir*—Sade argues that the Revolution will fail if it does not
push forward to a total unrepression of manners and morals. The
revolution must attain a state of permanent insurrection which is
by definition a state of immorality. As Sade claims: "l'état *moral*
d'un homme est un état de paix et de tranquillité, au lieu que
son état *immoral* est un état de mouvement perpétuel qui le
rapproche de l'insurrection nécessaire, dans laquelle il faut que le
républicain tienne toujours le gouvernement dont il est mem-
bre."[8] All of Sade's legislative project derives from this premise
that the morality of the Republic is immorality, and that one
must pursue the premise to its logical consequences, allowing all
desires a full field for their exercise. Why marriage, since all
children should be, not members of a family, but "uniquement
les enfants de la patrie?" (218). Incest? Does anything in nature
outlaw it? On the contrary. "J'ose assurer, en un mot, que
l'inceste devrait être la loi de tout gouvernement dont la fraternité
fait la base" (222). Sodomy? "L'habitude que les hommes ont de
vivre ensemble dans les républiques y rendra toujours ce vice plus
fréquent . . ." (225). At the climax of his argument, Sade reaches
the "singular reflection" that an old and corrupt nation that
throws off the yoke of tyranny can only maintain itself by crime:
"car elle est déjà dans le crime, et si elle voulait passer du crime à
la vertu, c'est-à-dire d'un état violent dans un état doux, elle
tomberait dans une inertie dont sa ruine serait bientôt le résultat"
(235). One recognizes here a kind of hyper-logical extension of
Robespierre's and Saint-Just's discourse of the necessity of Terror,
carried into an inner realm.

Sade's fierce logic constitutes a charge, which perhaps can
never be answered, against any political revolution: that it will
remain superficial, and hence ultimately unsatisfying to the
humanity it claims to benefit, if it does not address the liberation
of what lies in the psychic prisons—what Sade does not hesitate

to call the *crimes* of love. This critique of revolution was well captured for our own time by Peter Weiss' play, *The Persecution and Assassination of Jean-Paul Marat as Performed by the Inmates of the Asylum of Charenton under the Direction of the Marquis de Sade*. In this imagined debate between Marat and Sade, Sade finally argues the irreducible importance of the individual body and its desires: "Marat/ as I sat there in the Bastille/ for thirteen long years/ I learned/ that this is a world of bodies/ each body pulsing with a terrible power/ each body alone and racked with its own unrest/ In that loneliness/ marooned in a stone sea/ I heard lips whispering continually/ and felt all the time/ in the palms of my hands and in my skin/ touching and stroking/ Shut behind thirteen bolted doors/ my feet fettered/ I dreamed only/ of the orifices of the body/ put there/ so one may hook and twine oneself in them." Sade goes on to say: "Marat/ these cells of the inner self/ are worse than the deepest stone dungeon/ and as long as they are locked/ all your Revolution remains/ only a prison mutiny/ to be put down/ by corrupted fellow-prisoners."[9]

In Peter Weiss's remarkable recreation of Sade, we have the paradox made explicit: that it is in the deepest dungeon that one discovers the existence and the meaning of the psychic crypt, the inner spaces of claustration—*diese Gefängnisse des Innern*—which harbor drives that political Revolution ignores—and ignores at its peril, since political liberation may in fact stumble upon the possibility of, and perhaps the need for, another kind of liberation, one that politics cannot address, and which indeed threatens to deconstruct the whole meaning of political revolution. Only in prison is the truly revolutionary potential of the psyche and the body set at large. It is notable how close to Weiss' troubling vision some of the plays of the Revolution and its aftermath come, particularly Monvel's *Les Victîmes cloîtrées* and Pixerécourt's *Latude*. For if these are ostensibly plays about the liberation from political and social tyranny, they are, in their darker aspect, equally about what one finds when one goes to perform liberation from the space of claustration. What one finds is deeply disturbing, the content of those inner psychic cells that both demands liberation, and—from the point of view of the political—must not be liberated. The body cloistered, imprisoned, constrained is not a political body alone. It is a sexualized body, dreaming of its orifices, a body in a state of insurrection against the psychic mechanisms of repression and sublimation. The political sense of imprisonment in the Bastille is matched by the psychic and bodily meanings of confinement in the madhouse of Charenton.

I will give the last word to one of the Revolutionary party, to Saint-Just, who, in a famous line of his "Institutions républicaines," exclaims: "Le gouvernement républicain a la vertu pour principe; sinon, la terreur. Que veulent ceux qui ne veulent ni vertu ni terreur?"[10] What do they want, indeed? Saint-Just uses the logic of melodrama, the exclusion of the middle ground. But somewhere between republican virtue and republican terror lies a denied space that clamors for attention, and satisfaction.

NOTES

1. Victor Brombert, *La Prison romantique* (Paris, 1975).

2. The archeological model is omnipresent in Freud. See in particular, "Delusions and Dreams in Jensen's *Gradiva*," *The Standard Edition of the Complete Psychological Works* (London, 1953), vol. 9.

3. See Edmond Estève, "Le Théâtre 'monacal' sous la Révolution," *Etudes de littérature préromantique* (Paris, 1923), 83-137; also Robert Shackleton, "The Cloister Theme in French Preromanticism," in *The French Mind*, ed. Will Moore, Rhoda Sutherland, Enid Starkie (Oxford, 1952), 170-186; and the classic studies: Henri Welschinger, *Le Théâtre de la Révolution* (Paris, 1881) and Marvin A. Carlson, *The Theatre of the French Revolution* (Ithaca, 1966).

4. See Jean Starobinski, *1789: The Emblems of Reason*, trans. Barbara Bray (Carlottesville, 1982), chapter 5. On Pinel, see the very interesting study by Jan Goldstein, *Console and Classify: The French Psychiatric Profession in the Nineteenth Century* (Cambridge, 1987), chapter 3.

5. M.G. Lewis, *Venoni, or the Novice of St. Mark's* (London, 1809), v.

6. For a list of translations and adaptations, see Estève, "Le Théâtre 'monacal,' " 121-22.

7. Matthew Gregory Lewis, *The Monk*, ed. Lewis F. Peck (New York, 1959), 347. Subsequent references will be given in parentheses in the text.

8. D.A.F. de Sade, *La Philosophie dans le boudoir* (Paris, 1972), 208.

9. Peter Weiss, *Marat/Sade*, trans. Geoffrey Skelton and Adrian Mitchell (New York, 1966), 130-31; *Die Verfolgung und Ermordung Jean Paul Marats dargestellt durch die Schauspielgruppe des Hospizes zu Charenton unter Anleitung des Hernn de Sade* (Frankfurt, 1965).

10. Louis de Saint-Just, "Institutions républicaines," in *Oeuvres choisies* (Paris, 1968), 327.

FRENCH ROMANTIC HISTORIES OF THE REVOLUTION: MICHELET, BLANC, TOCQUEVILLE—A NARRATIVE

Linda Orr

Dans ce silence tout me déconcerte; des contradictions si étonnantes, des commencements si héroïques, des promesses si magnanimes et de tels mécomptes, comment les accorder? Encore si ces chutes n'étaient arrivées qu'une fois, mais on en peut compter plusieurs de ce genre en un demi-siècle. Elles ne sont donc pas un accident, mais un élément de notre société nouvelle.

Edgar Quinet

In nineteenth-century historiography, narrative appears to correspond to a teleological view of time. History lines up from a beginning through the present to an ultimate end. We have come to associate this history in particular with the political event, the points which organize the whole. If the eighteenth century set history on its course of progress, romantic historiography laid down not just any beginnings and ends but the origin and culmination of modern history, if not human time. The French Revolution was often the crux of this historical system. The teleological function of the revolution was so central to Michelet, for instance, that his history was described with a radical Christian metaphor as "messianic."[1]

At the same time, history added to narrative that discourse of truth or analysis and explanation. The problem of origins and ends got mixed up in this attempt to mark a difference within the discourse of narrative. This difference was not such an easy proposition to bring about, yet it was and still is crucial to the success of what may indeed have consequences for modern historical and scientific traditions.

The contemporary French historian, François Furet, while uncovering the artifice and especially the ideological burden of romantic narrative, brings under greater scrutiny the notion of teleology that functions in these texts. In *Penser la Révolution* (1978), Furet considers the special relationship in revolutionary history between narrative and analytic functions. Analysis was associated with the "origins" or "causes" of the Revolution. Then the narrative per se began with the "events," usually in 1787 or 1789, and finished at 9 Thermidor or 18 Brumaire. This

123

device produced the following effect: "comme si, une fois données les causes, la pièce allait toute seule, mue par l'ébranlement initial."[2] Furet implies that such an internal distinction of "genres" is rhetorical and does not necessarily represent a distinction between explanatory and narrative modes of discourse. But he does not pursue just how significant this rhetorical gesture of division is. Nor does he consider the consequences for the status of explanation itself.

The section Louis Blanc literally calls "Origins and Causes" in his *Histoire de la Révolution française* does not depend upon explanation as much as it simply prolongs the narrative backwards. The farther back into time, the better. According to this liberal strategy, practiced already in Restoration history, the Revolution gained a momentum of legitimacy by assimilating the march of time. Blanc began with the sixteenth-century religious wars; Michelet with the medieval church; Cabet with the Roman conquest of Gaul. No matter how far back it reaches, the explanation, as Furet observed, concludes and steps aside for the dramatic story. The differentiating, rhetorical gesture—which corresponds as well to periodization—distinguishes narrative from analysis and thus draws the distinction upon which the sense of that history depends. The arbitrary but necessary differentiation between causes and events or causes and effects completes the installation of a synecdochic system of truth. This small, almost automatic gesture, which we cannot avoid, constitutes temporality from which we make our categories of reality, along with the category of reality itself.[3] Periodization, the structure of historical narrative, is not then simply a matter of organizing data but of producing them. The rhetorical difference between explanation and narrative that engenders romantic history is reactivated throughout these texts.

The end or beginning of a chapter or section is often entitled "jugements historiques" or "critiques historiques" (see Blanc, Lamartine). As summaries, no more or less moralizing than the rest of the narrative, they provide a place of rest or of paralysis from which the entire edifice can supposedly be viewed, if not yet understood or explained. The central plot revolves around Parisian politics, more specifically Parisian parliaments, i.e., the speech and language of politics. Two major subplots—military and provincial history or the foreign and civil wars—shuffle in at conventional "frequencies"[4] so that the reader can always juggle the whole. Macro-histories (economic, geographical, cultural) and micro-histories (the press, the judicial system) are also interspersed at regular intervals. These ingenious structures could compete in architectural complexity with Proust. And they also have practical consequences: intricate sociotexts,[5] these histories are working out social and political hierarchies as well as hierarchies of knowledge and meaning.

The largest order of these narratives is tripartite. The trinity always emerges, as subtitle and section head: Assemblée constituante, Assemblée législative, and Convention, like a syllogism or Dialectic.

If the numerous possibilities for the origin dim already that origin's prestige, its narrative and explanatory authority, the end and culminating event presented, still presents, even more difficulty. Furet participates in that important tradition of revolutionary historiography that wants to "end the Revolution"—ever renewable tradition, keeping the Revolution more alive perhaps than those who want to continue it.[6] The latter make up a tradition that was evident as early as Babeuf and continued with Cabet, Guizot, Michelet, et al. to Soboul and beyond. For them, the revolution barely misses its mark each time, but is always eagerly awaited: 1830? 1848? 1870? 1914? 1936? 1968?

Not so purely teleological after all, romantic history is constructed upon a paradox or even tautology, rather than upon logic and the affirmation of progress. Such a historical system self-constitutes its own origin and end, its own referentiality and legitimacy, its own conclusions. Operating within an autonomous homogeneity, it defends itself against any "points" of difference. This implies, first, that the history known for its dependence on events leaves the very notion of event unmotivated, putting the idea of a telos into question. Second, and more serious, these romantic histories turn within their own undifferentiated narrative space (just as, according to Furet, jacobinism turned within its own imaginary sociopolitical space), from which emerges, nevertheless, a possibility of critical perspective but into which this critique is submerged again. Although our models of knowledge and history still work off of the genetic, teleogical tradition, the contradictory tendencies within this tradition become so disruptive that we must ask whether these disturbing elements are not constitutive and necessary to such a model or if one must modify or relinquish the model per se? Are we speaking about another kind of history?

I want to read the system of (jacobin) romantic narrative as if it represents neither a defect, an accident in historical practice, nor the neglected leftist political tradition of France, but rather the condition from which historico-realistic literature is written (and where it cannot help but "end up"). Furet draws a crucial distinction between two modes of history-writing, which—for the sake of polemics—he attaches to the figures of Michelet and Tocqueville:

> Il me semble que les historiens de la Révolution ont et ne cesseront d'avoir le choix entre Michelet et Tocqueville: ce qui ne veut pas dire entre une histoire républicaine et une histoire conservatrice de la Révolution française—puisque ces deux histoires seraient encore nouées par une problématique commune, que précisement Tocqueville récuse. Ce qui les sépare est ailleurs: c'est que Michelet fait revivre la Révolution de l'intérieur, Michelet communie, commémore, alors que Tocqueville ne cesse d'interroger l'écart qu'il soupçonne entre les intentions des acteurs et le rôle historique qu'ils jouent. Michelet s'installe dans la transparence révolutionnaire, il célèbre la coincidence mémorable entre les valeurs, le peuple et l'action des hommes. Tocqueville ne se borne pas à mettre en question cette transparence, ou cette coincidence. Il pense qu'elles masquent une opacité maximale entre l'action humaine et son sens réel, opacité caractéristique de la Révolutioon comme période historique, de par le rôle qu'y joue l'idéologie démocratique. (30-31)

The two "sides" become caricatures by virtue of the comparison. Michelet, the priest, communes mystically, i.e., uncritically, with the spirits of the Revolution, whereas the always questioning and suspicious Tocqueville alone "thinks . . . ." But Furet intends, in this way, to shift the debate from the context of ideology (whether liberal conservative vs. republican, republican vs. socialist, Girondist vs. Babeuf, non-Marxist vs. Marxist) to the relationship of the historian to his object, i.e., to his text.[7] Taking all these texts seriously, one may have difficulty in the end isolating the "Tocquevillian" alternative from the contradictory "Micheletist" history that covers up the opacity of Revolutionary discourse by celebrating its transparence. The nineteenth-century historians reanimate or repeat jacobin strategies or the jacobin problematic, for it may well convey a basic gesture of history, or at least of our Western history so wrapped up in revolution. Nineteenth-century historians advertised loudly their own lucidity, which depended in large measure upon making the break of periodization stick and thus having constantly to remake it anew—which only muddied by such internal tensions that ever proud lucidity.

It is not only possible but necessary for these histories both to promote adamantly the origins per se, and to panic, hesitate, cover up, dance around an infinitely postponed gesture that would fix that teleological system of truth. This discrepancy may create another kind of *écart* than the one Furet describes. Does Tocqueville's capacity to focus on the *écart* in Revolutionary practice provide him, in turn, with that *écart* or distance necessary for the practice of analytic history? The discrepancies in Revolutionary ideology, accumulating in historiographical practice (or vice versa), may contribute to that more visible impression of a confusion between action and intention or action and consequences, that is, between action and its sense. But those paradoxes or duplicities within politico-historiographical practice, less clearly identifiable than those more traditional oppositions (action/intention etc.), interject there an element of slippage that plays havoc with the teleological system while not being able to do without it.

My study of romantic narratives[8] concentrates here on Michelet, since he provides the institutionally-acceptable[9] edge from which to pass into less familiar territory, and on Louis Blanc, since he best incarnates the neo-jacobin tradition.[10] Like his contemporaries (e.g., Cabet) Blanc has only been studied, if at all, in terms of social or political history or even more rarely, in histories of history. (And who fills in the nineteenth-century blank of Furet's category when, in the end, Furet saves Michelet from the category he defined?) Generalizing from close readings, I read a "new" history emerging that these historians perhaps cannot say and yet connive with us readers to represent. However, I am also aware that this essay should be about how hard it is to separate "old" from "new" and to generalize in the first place.

Michelet's Genealogy of History

In the introduction to his *Histoire de la Révolution française*, Michelet immediately considers the problems of relationship, i.e., of historical periodization, which he discusses, awkwardly and brilliantly, in both "logical" and "historical" terms at the same time. Justice-Revolution and Grace-Christianity can be read as ideals manifest in material history, whose constant oppositon is, nonetheless, dissolved at both the beginning and end of this history.

The famous sentence of the introduction, and its re-writings, provide an aphorism or enigma, instead of a definition, to which the Introduction and the history keep referring in order to give it the effect of a definition:

Je définis la Révolution, l'avènement de la Loi, la résurrection du Droit, la
réaction de la Justice.

La Révolution n'est autre chose que la réaction tardive de la Justice contre le
gouvernement de la faveur et la religion de la Grâce.

Qu'est-ce que la Révolution? La réaction de l'équité, l'avènement tardif de la
Justice éternelle.[11]

While the Christian metaphors, such as advent and resurrec-
tion, strike at first the reader's attention, Michelet finally uses the
more neutral or polyvalent "reaction" most often. The Revolution not only rises as if from nowhere, but in response to another
system, called Grace. But "reaction" does not clarify that
response: Justice might be a return to an anterior state, might
always (atemporally) oppose Grace, or represent, as in the
chemical connotation of the word, any interchange between two
substances. The creeping insistence on the word "tardy" implies,
not only that Justice is late in declaring its eternal dominion, but
that Justice is eternally late—that the only eternal quality Justice
possesses is its lateness.

The enigmatic definition leads quickly to the question: "la
Révolution est-elle chrétienne, anti-chrétienne?" And, just as
quickly, the historian, without limiting the importance of the
question itself, acknowledges the strategic or theoretical signifi-
cance of being able to answer or pose that question in the first
place. "Cette question, historiquement, logiquement, précède
toute autre." The question has two simultaneous branches. First,
Michelet asks how the new principle can be described in relation
to the old one: "Celui que va raconter la crise où le nouveau
principe surgit et se fit sa place, ne peut se dispenser de lui
demander ce qu'il est par rapport à son aîné, en quoi il le
continue, en quoi il le dépasse, le domine ou l'abolit. Grave
problème que personne n'a encore envisagé face à face" (21-22).
The question of principle can also be restated as a practical one.
Simply: what verbs does the historian use to shape his periods:
continue, go beyond, dominate, abolish? Do these proposed
solutions contradict the fiat (se fit) of a "rising up" of the "new,"
ex nihilo? Somehow no one else ever seems to ask this basic
question that Michelet (always alone) uncovers. Others either act
as if it has already been resolved or as if it is merely "une
question accessoire" (23). On the contrary, writes Michelet, no
history can be written until this problem is reckoned with.
Another or the other part of the question concerns whether there
are one or two historical objects (one or two questions?):

"Historien de la Révolution, je ne puis, sans cette recherche, faire même un seul pas. [. . .] La misérable connivence où restent les deux partis est une des causes dominantes de notre affaiblissement moral. Combat de condottieri, où personne ne combat. [. . .] Tant que les questions fondamentales restent ainsi éludées, il n'y a nul progrès à espérer, ni religieux, ni social. [. . .] Mais jamais dans le faux, dans le ruse, dans les traités du mensonge, ne peut commencer la foi." (24). It was convenient for the "condottieri" (Italian mercenary soldiers) as Michelet refers to both the political (parlementary) and religious (Jesuitical) orders of the day, to connive together. Although a political and social revolution was supposed to have happened, Michelet asks if it simply reshuffled (political) structures already developed by the Church, and did the Church still hold the "historical base" of power? The word "connivance" frequently privileged in both the introduction and Michelet's work in general, evokes the image of eyes half-closed (trying to stay open or closed?) with the added connotation of the wink. Connivers have one eye open and one closed, for they pretend not to see the wrongdoing they sanction by this very pretense, and they conveniently cannot be accused of this (inadvertent?) sanction. Finally, the transition that Michelet brings off at the end of this paragraph between historiographical strategy and historico-political (or moral) strategies appears less naive when one considers that both practices respond to similar questions, summarized perhaps too broadly as what makes modern society cohere. Whatever gives the historical narrative sense may also be working to keep the socio-historical institutions in operation.

A rather astounding passage follows in which Michelet resolves, with an almost sleight-of-hand, that "grave problem" no one had heretofore even posed:

> Si la Révolution était cela, rien de plus, elle ne serait pas distincte du Christianisme. . . . Elle ne serait rien en elle-méme. En ce cas, il n'y aurait pas deux acteurs, mais un seul, le Christianisme. S'il n'y a qu'un acteur, il n'y a un point de drame, point de crise; la lutte que nous croyons voir est une pure illusion. . . .
>
> Mais non, il n'en est pas ainsi. La lutte n'est que trop réelle. Ce n'est pas ici un combat simulé entre le méme et le même. Il y a deux combattants.
>
> Et il ne faut pas dire non plus que le principe nouveau n'est que'une critique de l'ancien, un doute, une pure négation. —Qui a vu une négation? Qu'est-ce qu'une négtion vivante . . . ?
>
> Donc, il y a deux choses . . . l'ancien, le nouveau. [. . .] Il faut sortir des malentendus, si l'on veut savoir où l'on va. (25)

The circular reasoning embellishes a tautological syllogism. It is almost as simple as saying that if the Revolution was an extension of Christianity, then it would not exist; but it exists and therefore it is not an extension of Christianity. The circularity is troubling since the decisive factor—whether there is drama, crisis, battle, i.e., actual antagonism, or not—represents what was previously being questioned: the "combat de condottieri." He uses as the turning point in his argument the denial of the original question: how can we tell a simulated from a real combat, a simulated from a real Revolution? In fact, the very outrageousness of the reasoning implies that it hardly matters how one breaks through an unresolvable question, this rhetorical barrier, before beginning a history (or society based on faith); what matters is to state that there are two objects and get on with it. The process is somehow reversed in that the initial presupposition appears as the consequence: "Il faut sortir des malentendus. . . . " In order to get out of the cycle of arbitrary misunderstandings in which we cannot distinguish between two conniving parties, we posit the possibility, even the necessity of the distinction between the two, one of which is named the "old," and the other, Justice. With this distinction made (as the process of signification arbitrarily differentiates signs that we take for granted, or as metaphorical language is resolved into the two terms of comparison in order to be explained), the historian can then proceed to build his argument upon that unquestioned cleavage of comparison itself: "Voilà toute la ressemblance. Et voici la différence" (25). History can then be written.

But Michelet's text also connives with itself because it both is written and yet never gets beyond the question it sets out to answer. After trying to work out his "grave problem" through a syllogistic logic, Michelet will appear to turn toward different manifestations of "story" in order to provide a form of explanation (aphorism, genealogy, fable, the long historical narrative). But even in this progression, it is hard to say where logic ends and timeless or timely story begins or which comes first. Each seems equally inadequate without the others. The (logical) principles of Michelet's history can only be explained in the story, eventually the long narrative, which would not make sense without the frame of these originally confused and illogically related principles. One might also conclude, with some regret, that the mode of discourse does not in fact change when it passes from the fables (or even the "logic") of the

introduction to the seven-volumed history of events. The reader
learns nothing in the seven volumes he does not know from the
introduction. And yet, these volumes, besides telling the story in
a long form that was conventionally pleasing to the audience of
that time, are necessary to the success of the project. The weighty
body of the text retrospectively proves the logic of the
introduction by erecting an undeniable revolution, by miming
the monument it constructs. Even at this outlandish proportion,
this history keeps telling the story of how the (real) Revolution
has not arrived, perhaps cannot arrive. That is, it is still not sure
if it can tell the difference between the Old Regime's false
revolutions and the promise of the new. History—both senses of
the word—still cannot take that first step.

  L'Histoire de la Révolution française performs the very
historical problematic whose repetitions keep it moving, for
Michelet must define the (new) Revolution within the (old)
prevalent Christian system; he must find the cultural equivalent
of the teleological narrative structure. Is this why readers dismiss
Michelet too easily, read him too literally? One can no more
extract those Christian figures from his language than one could
extract figure itself from language, Hegel from Marx, Roman
virtue from eighteenth-century Revolutionary discourse.

  Consider the genealogy of Grace and Justice at the beginning
of Michelet's introduction. On the one hand, it looks as if Justice
is the very term precluded by the system (of Grace), which works
by definition on the exclusion of Justice and cleverly bars its
eventual return by perverting all of its possible forms of
expression. One cannot get there from here, i.e., to Justice from
Grace. "Parti de l'arbitraire, ce système doit rester dans
l'arbitraire, il n'en peut sortir d'un pas" (29). And yet, on the
other hand, Justice has only to be itself to reverse the mock
sovereignty of Grace: "Pour que la Justice [. . .] se hasarde à
relever la tête, il faut une chose difficile (tant le sens humain est
étouffé sous la pesanteur des maux et la pesanteur des siècles), il
faut que la Justice recommence à se croire juste, qu'elle s'éveille,
se souvienne d'elle-méme, reprenne conscience du droit" (30).
Justice simply has to recognize itself for what it is: just. But
doesn't that mean that Justice is gratuitous, and is known, not by
any of its (false) definitions as "Grace," but only by self-identity
in tautology itself—that is, finally as the true principle of Grace?
The system still operates, then, according to a double-bind or
irony in which Grace can only be read as Justice and Justice's

only name is Grace. And such paradoxes would keep history turning into its other and (never) starting over again: something other than teleology or ontology. Unteleology? Untology?

Michelet's text can be read both teleologically and unteleologically. He keeps trying to re-establish the "line" (between the "old" regime and "new" revolution, between Grace and Justice) that slips, multiplies and finally keeps already being effaced before he can begin to secure it. Tocqueville works curiously toward a similarly duplicitous history from the other direction. He keeps trying to erase the lines, especially that all-important one of 1789, that he must, nevertheless, continue to draw elsewhere in order to make sense of his narrative. One must be careful to follow the differences as Michelet's break keeps slipping away from him and as Tocqueville's erased line keeps reappearing, but one can also see a similarity in the historical systems both imply. *"Voici la ressemblance."* Michelet's system of Grace transfers itself from the medieval ecclesiastical courts of law, to the Monarchy's arbitrary justice, and to the Terror's false revolution. The Old Regime system of centralization and homogeneity is constantly displaced in Tocqueville from the emergence of Roman law in Europe, to the growing central administration of the Monarchy, and to its extension in the "imaginary" revolution. For both, Justice or liberty keeps escaping to the limits of a system in which it can only be read as what is excluded and yet whose promise and reality keep that system in constant circulation. Both try to refer back to a historical precedent from which they can predict the possibility of Justice or liberty's return (for Michelet, the Roman tradition of Justice; for Tocqueville, what is supposedly just the opposite, the common law tradition). But both define Justice or liberty precisely by the impossibility of getting logically, by links, by cause and effect, from the one system to the other, although recognizing that the "antagonists" are strangely interdependent, i.e., connive. Both historians spend, therefore, most of the space of their histories, nonetheless permeated with the desire and poetry of liberty, with a similar analysis of the tenuous and yet resistant strategies of the system in place—that are, oddly enough, the very strategies of its competition as well. For both, the reversals, which are prepared "ecclesiastically" in Michelet, like a subterranean supplanting in Tocqueville (like Marx's grubbing mole), can never be read until they are already complete.

But despite the affinities of structure (and differences of content)[12] between Michelet (his jacobin-romantic colleagues) and

Tocqueville, why do we naturally perceive them as opposites? *"Et voici la différence."* Which is purely rhetorical? Michelet's discourse sounds crazy to us, while Tocqueville's is analytical and lucid. Besides considering the ideologies of reading, we might also entertain the hypothesis that Michelet's "madness" (as if Tocqueville's excruciating logic is any less mad) serves as strategy. Does Michelet think he will get away with his outrageous ambition of inscribing Justice or the Revolution (within the linguistic and historical system of Grace) by appearing to speak folly (obviously common sense if we would only wake up)? Or does he invite our devastating criticism and a kind of sadistic mockery, himself a masochist? Both Michelet and Tocqueville, along with their contemporaries, wanted to right the revolution of liberty, instead of re-instituting its idolatry, and yet neither could predict how he would be read.

Louis Blanc and the History of Anticipated Dis-appointment

Louis Blanc's *Histoire de la Révolution française*, a stereotype of (jacobin) romantic historiography, not only fits—too well— Furet's description of the genre, but prolongs a discourse alternating between paranoia and pathos, hysteria and lyricism, for twelve volumes: the record for this nineteenth-century corpus (except for Buchez and Roux's forty volumes of "documents"). Supposedly simplistic passages, wheeling out the clichés of romantic history, especially the binaries of cause and event, of idea and material history, are made more bothersome by categorical pronouncements exaggerating the usual didacticism, and by a plot held together with the milky consistency of melodrama.

Blanc, applying his Hegel, announces, in a short preamble to his Introduction, that history is structured according to three "principles" (thus differing from the more binary divisions of Michelet or Tocqueville): "Trois grands principes se partagent le monde et l'histoire: L'AUTORITE, L'INDIVIDUALISME, LA FRATERNITE."[13] Each stage develops out of proportion until it inverts into its opposite. After Authority decided questions according to blind belief and superstitious tradition, Individualism introduced rationalism which "poussé à l'excès, se dénonçait lui-même" in the form of intellectual anarchism. Fraternity was conceived as bringing back a principle of solidarity, this time, however, based on consensus, "sur la persuasion, sur la volontaire assentiment des coeurs." But Blanc's text evokes, rather than consistently applies, this tripartite (Dialectical?) order, that was also broadly disseminated in French texts not overtly influenced by Hegel. In fact another structure, more reminiscent of Michelet and Tocqueville, also emerges in which the rise and triumph of the Bourgeoisie (like Michelet's Monarchy or Tocqueville's old regime-centralization-&-equality) leave little room on either edge for Authority or Fraternity. The Monarchy is only interesting as the site of the "lutte . . . sourde" in which the Bourgeoisie is already profiting from whatever maneuvers the Monarchy thought benefited it. And Fraternity is the desired, perhaps impossible element of Blanc's history, like Michelet's Justice, Tocqueville's liberty, present already in the unreadable future: "Sous cette surface, l'idée immortelle, l'indomptable idée de la France poursuit son cours, et lorsqu'elle reparaît, on est surpris de tout le chemin qu'elle fait, quand pas un signe visible, pas un bruit perceptible, ne trahissaient son mouvement" (1:562). Of course this repeats again the dilemma of the historian who wishes not to celebrate in reverse the (Bourgeois) system already in place—i.e., to lament, while charting, its miraculous survival—but rather to reveal the necessary coming of the (second) revolution. Less explicitly than Tocqueville, Blanc also suggests that there is perhaps no other alternative for the historian than to mirror the present authority, whose repetitions as past or future, as "surface glacée" block or freeze the future or past one would rather read. Is Blanc's frustration, exacerbated at times to hysteria, more understandable when one sees him running again and again into this impenetrable, and yet delusive, surface?

The rhetorical or generic division of Blanc's history into "Origins and Causes" followed by the supposedly motivated events of the narrative should correspond as well to a shift in the evolution of the three principles. His "Origins . . . " trace the rise of Bourgeois Individualism from within ecclesiastical-monarchic Authority, and the body of the narrative recounts the parallel emergency of Fraternity from within Bourgeois Individualism. However, Fraternity fails to emerge. The two parts of Blanc's history might, instead, be described as the playful logic of pre-revolutionary history followed by a class-less, or homogeneously Bourgeois, unprincipled state called the "noir imbroglio" of the Revolution.

The problem comes from living that frustrating paradox in which no one can read what will have, retrospectively, already been proven logical. Blanc expresses, then, opposing points of view on this history that appears or is made to appear both capricious and methodically systematic. On the one hand, he, like Michelet, incorporates a conspiracy into the logico-historical beginning of his narrative. On the other hand, he, also like Michelet, presents the story of the conspiracy as a way of illustrating a less determinable, constitutive problem in history. Just as for Michelet Grace had slipped into the guise of Justice, for Blanc Individualism triumphs by committing inequities in the name of liberty. When one looks closer, the three principles, as "arid" as Blanc thought their definitions were, already inscribe, despite the effect of their syllogistic logic, a snagged development. "Liberté! avait dit Luther, liberté! ont répété en choeur les philosophes du dix-huitième siècle; et c'est le mot liberté qui, de nos jours, est écrit sur la bannière de la civilisation. Il y a là malentendu et mensonge; et, depuis Luther, ce malentendu, ce monsonge ont rempli l'histoire; c'était l'individualisme qui arrivait, et non la liberté" (1:xxix). In the beginning was an ambiguous take-over; mistake or ruse? This creates a kind of logical impasse: how can the true proponents of liberty declare the advent of their principle when people think that they have been living in liberty all this time? What can they call *their* principle, how can they know it? It was a little absurd to accuse the Bourgeoisie (Richelieu or Louis XIV) of maliciously plotting to get where they did not know they were going. "La bourgeoisie elle-même, dans sa course ardente vers la domination absolue, n'avait qu'un sentiment confus de son oeuvre, et elle était loin de croire que rendre la royauté indépendante, c'était l'abolir. Mais, je le répète, les hommes sont presque toujours les jouets des choses qu'ils accomplissent. Les sociétés vivent sur un malentendu éternel."[14] In this passage from Blanc's *Histoire de dix ans* (1842), the word *malentendu*, whose recurrence in his work will become more obvious, generalizes the predicament (while still including the possibility of lies). From one point of view (their own?) the bourgeoisie was muddling around, while from another (history's) it was racing toward absolute domination. Blanc pauses at this striking aphorism—societies live on (according to, on the basis of) an eternal misunderstanding. They are founded, curiously, upon a condition of impaired hearing. They cannot be sure of where exactly they are as they nonetheless rush there as if driven by an order.

The result is the "noir imbroglio" of the Revolution as narrated in Blanc's remaining eleven volumes, for the Bourgeoisie already drops out around 1789 (with Lafayette, Mounier, Bailly, Sieyès, Lally-Tollendal). (Is this because everything is now bourgeois? The class analysis, presented with relatively sophisticated definitions, falls away.) And the "utopian-socialist" historian must fill the dark space between the completed empire and the invisibility of the new one. It can be argued that Blanc, at this point, gives us a revolution from the inside where no one, including the well-intentioned Robespierre, can read what is going on. From the twisting syllogisms, Blanc resorts to the repetitions of parody and farce as if not even absurd syllogisms can be unraveled from the melee anymore. Both ridiculous and tragic imitations of the desired system—liberty, democracy, the people, fraternity—pile up: the Girondists, "artistes égarés dans la politique," donned red bonnets and promoted the joke "sans culotte," while Hébertists dressed up (affubla) their doctrine "in rags" and "lui donna à parler le langage des halles . . . " (2:363). And, all the time, each manifestation of the mask accuses the others of disguise: "Il y eut un moment où Paris devint la ville aux mascarades, et cela tout en criant: A bas les momeries!" (2:367). The chapter titles in Blanc outdo even Lamartine in their evocation of trickery, mystery, blindness, confusion, madness, and titillating horror: "Emeute factice," "frayeurs simulées," "frauduleuses démarches des fauteurs d'émeutes," "fausses rumeurs," "ce qu'il y avait de louche . . . ," "Artifices pieux," "aveuglement des deux partis en lutte," "la trompette du jugement dernier sonnée . . . ," "Paris en délire," "monstres produits par le règne du meurtre," "ce qui est sorti de cet accouplement abominable." So how could the Revolution avoid making mistakes and errors? "Enveloppée par l'intrigue et la trahison comme par une nuit épaisse, et forcée de combattre des ennemis qu'elle n'aperçut le plus souvent qu'à la lueur des éclairs, il lui arriva sans nul doute d'égarer ses coups sur des innocents; mais ceux-là mêmes, elle ne les frappa que parce qu'elle eut le malheur de les croire coupables" (2:383). The obsessive thematics of the Revolution's errancy—where it went wrong, went off course,[15] got lost—returns in the verb égarer. The Revolution, égarée itself, lost control of its own defensive blows and struck itself.

When the revolutionaries are blinded by their own experience, the historian is called in to see clearly: "Et c'est ce qui rend si délicat, disons mieux, si redoutable, la tâche de l'Histoire, sommée de voir clair dans ce noir imbroglio, et de démêler"

(2:525). Whereas Blanc, like his contemporaries, undertakes this task, does he not, in the meantime, write the more feasible novel of the national nightmare? "[T]elle est la tâche qu'il faut remplir pour faire comprendre une révolution qui ne nous apparaîtrait, sans cela, que comme le rêve sanglant d'un pays en délire" (1:cxlvii). When the principles and the class distinctions disappear, Blanc is left with the parody of that repeated delirium.

Blanc's *Histoire de la Révolution française* further breaks the illusion of eighteenth-century history speaking itself[16] by referring to contemporary, nineteenth-century events. In so doing, his history appears to anticipate solutions for eighteenth-century impasses, and yet it also turns those solutions back into the problems that called for them. (Does that mirror-effect set up, nonetheless, a kind of tautological explanatory system?[17]) The Revolution, was, therefore, blind to what *L'Organisation du travail* (1839) promises to provide (and fails to? i.e., the Revolution). Then the *Histoire de dix ans, 1830-1840* (1842) repeats, more profoundly, the blindness of the Revolution and the same unanswered call for social remedies. "Le renversement de la royauté suffirait-il pour rendre désormais impossible dans les relations civiles la tyrannie du capitaliste sur les travailleurs? . . . De telles questions étaient trop hautes pour l'époque et plus d'une tempête devait éclater avant gu'on songeât à les résoudre. En 1830 on ne songeait pas même à les poser." Even 1848 (and Blanc's *Histoire de la révolution de 1848*, 1870-1880) represented no progress, which, in an odd reversal, the post-1848 volumes of the *Histoire de la Révolution française* laments. "On sait ce qui eut lieu après la Revolution de 1848. Il aurait fallu organiser le travail: on ne sut qu'enrégimenter la misère" (1:214) In Blanc's written work, Blanc may well be referring to his disappointment when the Luxembourg Commission got no support from the provisional government of 1848 that set it up. The more one tries to bring about that magic formula, to organize work, the more one produces its other, a kind of inorganic, mechanical, or even military, reordering of the same poverty, the same travail.[18] On the one hand, Blanc predicts the second (socialist) revolution and the new (social) history of the Revolution (Soboul, et al.), that he knew himself not to have the equipment to accomplish. And Blanc the politician strives constantly to bring about that prediction. But on the other hand, he keeps inscribing in all of his histories a metaphorical space for future error: neither utopia nor dystopia ("utropia" perhaps).

So why does Blanc's text (and History) not come to terms with itself?

L'Histoire de la Révolution française does pause to reconsider itself at certain rhetorically-repetitive moments that, in retrospect, might have been predictable. These places, including the end of the second volume (of the original 12-volume edition, published in 1847), a reflection on the Terror (vol. 10), and the reaction to Robespierre's death, can be identified by a list of rhetorical questions or even exclamations that gesture toward a radical redefinition of history. But the question is hardly formulated when Blanc either answers it (rhetorically), represses it, or postpones it, implying that the answer depends upon the successful performance of his own book—the one answer his book cannot give.

This passage on the Terror most blatantly closes the opening that it has just made:

> Cependant, si, sous prétexte de salut public, vous frappez d'ostracisme Thémistocle; si vous proscrivez à perpétuité la famille d'un mauvais prince; si vous portez la main sur un innocent parce qu'il nous paraît dangereux, où sera la boussole de l'univers moral? Où sera le refuge contre l'iniquité, subitement devenue justice, en vertu du SALUT DU PEUPLE, qui aura été compris de telle ou telle manière et arbitrairement défini par des gouvernements de passage, infaillibles tant qu'ils sont debout, accusés d'imposture dès qu'ils sont par terre? . . .
>
> C'est que, sur tout ce débat, pèse un malentendu effroyable, et malheur à qui ne le signalerait pas, croyant l'avoir découvert! . . . dans la pratique, le SALUT DU PEUPLE veut toujours dire le SALUT D'UN PEUPLE. . . . Ne dites donc pas LE SALUT DU PEUPLE EST LA SUPREME LOI: dites: LE SALUT DE L'HUMANITE EST LA SUPREME LOI. Dès lors, plus de ténèbres. (1:487)

Blanc analyses the disfiguration of that most promising of phrases: salvation of the people. If Blanc avoids appearing to defend the enemy (Vergniaud, Philippe Egalité) by using the ancient Greek example of Themistocles, he brings up the problem his contemporaries (and ours) have cast in the same metaphor: if this sacred phrase can be used as the excuse for such crimes, "where is the moral compass?" Are we a ship tossing at sea or a walker lost in the dark woods? Michelet's genius-people made the mistake of seeking refuge, i.e., symbolic incarnation for this popular notion of public salvation and safety, but is the alternative of perpetual errancy and *égarement* any more acceptable? We are back in the fable of Justice and Grace. Iniquity appears in the guise of justice, by virtue (that loaded word in the context of the eighteenth-century jacobin Revolution) of these magic phrases whose prestige gives protection to the wrong camp. "Salut du peuple" is a captive to each succeeding government; it is defined "arbitrarily" by each passing authority that appears to know all until the next revolution when it is said to have been wrong and criminal.

Consequently, when we read the first sentence of the second paragraph, we expect a justification on the order of the "eternal misunderstanding." In fact the phrase, "thinking he discovered it" suggests the irony that only a naive researcher could believe he has "discovered" something so recurrent. But perhaps Blanc is not ironic at all. He continues by recommending, or rather ordering the substitution of one word by another as if the whole problem hinges simply on that. The figurative generality of "people" too easily covers up each nation's egotistical[19] desires. Blanc predicts that the frightful (terrorizing) misunderstanding would not subsist if the word "humanity" was used in its place. One feels the relief that follows this historical and rhetorical impasse, as if the doors of narrative swing open again (reminding us of Michelet's "il faut sortir des malentendus, si l'on veut savoir où l'on va"): "dès lors, plus de ténèbres." It is hard to believe, in the constantly re-enveloping night of Blanc's plot, that this conclusion is definitive.

In the passage closing the first two volumes of his *History* and published in 1847, Blanc adopts the other tactic. He suggests that he cannot answer the rhetorical questions except by postponing them, but he ends, in fact, by establishing another imperative which is, this time, more problematic, if equally authoritarian in tone.

> Mais le moment arrivait où les malentendus deviendraient manifestes. L'individualisme venait de donner sa formule: déjà la Fraternité laissait deviner la sienne.
>
> C'est pourquoi . . . une second révolution était inévitable. . . .
>
> Mais quoi! est-ce qu'une loi souveraine, une loi terrible n'a pas attaché le mal au bien comme une condition absolue, irrévocable? Qu'est-ce que l'univers animé? . . . Qu'est-ce que la vérité? . . . Dans la nature, les espèces ne subsistent que par la destruction des espèces inférieures.
>
> Ne vous hâtez pas de conclure! L'ardente, l'invincible protestation qui sort des profondeurs de la conscience humaine, voilà ce qui mentre que la NECESSITE DU MAL est un mensonge. La dignité de l'homme consiste à le croire, sa puissance sera de le prouver. (1:182)

In such passages, Blanc often asks literally if there is a "law" to be deduced from the history that keeps writing itself in his book, despite himself.[20] The only way he can express the pattern (?) he keeps reading is in Christian terms (evil inseparable from good) or in fatalistic terms, cast here in uncannily Darwinian metaphors.[21] But no hypothesis really satisfies him, as he runs through the gamut yet another time. Here, Blanc does not have a quick solution, and he cautions against the practice of hasty conclusions that he, of course, in turn adopts elsewhere.

But leaving history in suspension is not the same as writing a history of suspended suspension, a history that would be constitutively inconclusive. The strategy arrived at in the last sentence could, however, only apply to a history whose results are still out. Lies like truths are constructed after the fact (instead of after or according to facts). The Necessity of Evil is not an a priori metaphysical hypothesis but the syllogistic proof man reads history into. The problem with this is that history is continually up for grabs. The only way that Blanc can finally prove the Necessity of Right in history is to bring about, by virtue of his history, the new society he inscribes as inevitable there. His book must "perform" the Revolution it predicts. Such a paradox comments on the aphorism Michelet rephrases in his famous 1869 Preface to the *Histoire de France* ("Man is his own Prometheus") as well as on similar statements by Marx that do not necessarily contradict his determinism either.

"An Element of Our New Society" and Its History

What is, then, the figure, are the figures, of history that emerge from this corpus or do not? And what is the status of these "jacobin-romantic" narratives that are neither self-conscious nor unconscious about their successes or failures? I am tempted to re-privilege in these works anticipations of their own self-deceptions, their own inevitable errors. But then I am only substituting another criterion for Furet's judgments (that place analysis over a mixed, unself-conscious narrative, Tocqueville and Quinet over Michelet and Blanc) or even for the more traditional ideological divisions. By emphasizing the rhetorical undertow of romantic narrative histories, my reading risks blurring important distinctions among them while trying to hear their specific dismay and passion.

What happens to that " Tocquevillian" alternative if we cannot escape the "jacobin-romantic" moment of simultaneous confusion and tirades of truth? Analysis continues to return to narrative and vice versa in the attempt to extract a point of view from the self-legitimating and self-destructing process associated with history, our culture's particular form of social self-expression. Analysis is not dropped. But neither is it possible or even recommendable to prolong the glimpses of "self-critique" which turn as quickly and as dangerously into another suggestion of how to institute the proper history better. For this would still be rejuvenating the system of Grace. Perhaps the only way of overcoming the "grave problem" is (to pretend) not to hear it while getting gingerly on with one's work, thereby ever commemorating the failure of that pretense or repression. Such a pragmatic coincides with the strategy of French romantic history, founder of our social and political sciences.

NOTES

1. The epigraph is from *La Révolution* (Paris, 1987), Collection "Littérature/ Politique," 163; see Claude Lefort's Preface.

2. (Paris), 34; subsequent references will be cited parenthetically in the text. See also Claude Lefort's "Penser la révolution dans la Révolution française," *Essais sur le politique (XIXè-XXè siècles)* (Paris, 1986).

3. See the introduction to Hayden White's *Metahistory: The Historical Imagination in Nineteenth-Century Europe* (Baltimore, 1973), especially 35-36: "And, by such reductions, as Vico, Hegel, and Nietzsche all pointed out, the phenomenal world can be populated with a host of agents and agencies that are presumed to exist *behind* it. Once the world of phenomena is separated into two orders of being (agents and causes on the one hand, acts and effects on the other), the primitive consciousness is endowed, *by purely linguistic means alone*, with the conceptual categories (agents, causes, spirits, essences) necessary for the theology, science, and philosophy of civilized reflection."

4. See Gérard Genette, *Narrative Discourse: An Essay in Method* (Ithaca, 1980), ch. 3. A more thorough and strictly technical narrative analysis of a historical text would be fruitful. Awaiting her book, see Ann Rigney's "Toward Varennes," in *New Literary History* 18 (1986-1987), 77-98.

5. My use of the word is influenced by French "socio-criticism" (see especially the work of Claude Duchet, and in the U.S. an issue of *Sub-Stance*, no. 15, 1976). Instead of paralleling, reflecting or opposing society, the text, as it works out complex social hierarchies, is producing or performing the society that will in turn appear to explain the text.

6. The first half of *Penser la Révolution* is entitled "La Révolution française est terminée." See also Furet's *Marx et la Révolution française: textes de Marx présentés, réunis, traduits par Lucien Calvié* (Paris, 1986), 88.

7. Furet's own book gets to a study of the French Revolution through the accumulated blindness of historiography. Perhaps without meaning to, Furet locates the practice of history in competing readings of historiography, rather than in truth-claims of the archive.

8. While trying to keep problems of "discourse" or "enunciation" at bay (i.e., within the text, signs of its own reading and writing procedures), they have at times been impossible to avoid, but acknowledging them may in fact preclude being able to discuss the texts, their structure, in the first place.

9. As well as Furet, see Soboul: "tradition progressiste de l'historiographie révolutionnaire, de Michelet à Lefebvre, en passant pas Jaurès, Aulard et

Mathiez . . . —la seule qui, dans la démarche de principe, ait été et demeure scientifique." Avant-propos to Claude Mazauriac's *Sur la Révolution française: Contributions à l'histoire de la révolution bourgeoise* (Paris, 1970), 6.

10. I am extending the term to define an inseparable element of nineteenth-century French society, as Gramsci does, instead of limiting it to the case of Isser Woloch's *Jacobin Legacy: The Democratic Movement Under the Directory* (Princeton, 1970).

11. Ed. Gérard Walter, 2 vols. (Paris, 1952), 1:21, 30, 76; subsequent references will be cited parenthetically in the text. To distinguish them from Michelet's, my ellipses are between brackets.

12. Sometimes, however, their content and very words are similar; the following description from Michelet, lamenting the disappearance of local traditions, anticipates Tocqueville's: "Plus de vie féodale ni de vie municipale; perdue dans la royauté. Plus de vie religieuse, eτteinte avec le clergé. Hélas! pas même de légendes locales, de traditions nationales, plus de ces heureux préjugés qui font la vie du peuple enfant. Ils ont tout détruit chez lui, jusqu'à ses erreurs" (1:55).

13. Blanc, *Histoire de la Révolution française* (Paris, s.d.), 1:xxix; quotations will henceforth come from this "popular," illustrated edition in two volumes and will be documented parenthetically in the text.

14. *Histoire de dix ans* (Paris, 1844), 1:79-80.

15. See chapter 5, "The Revolution Blown Off Course," in François Furet and Denis Richet's *French Revolution* (New York, 1970).

16. See Roland Barthes' essay "Historical Discourse," in Michael Lane's *Introduction to Structuralism* (New York, 1970), 145-155, rpt. from *Social Science Information* (August 1967). The same French text appears again in *Poétique*, 49 (Fév. 1982).

17. For a study of this strategy as represented in Flaubert's *Bouvard et Pécuchet*, see Françoise Gaillard, "An Unspeakable (Hi)story," *Yale French Studies* 59(1980):137-54.

18. The pun made possible by the different meanings of *travail* in French and in English ironically underscores Blanc's point. Cf. "Blanc's historical studies aroused within him a sense of travail, of bewilderment, and a fear of those too simple forumulas that lure men into fatal action," from Leo A. Loubère, *Louis Blanc: His Life and His Contribution to the Rise of French Jacobin-Socialism* (Evanston, Ill., 1961), 34.

19. The duplicitous application of the word *peuple* recalls both the secret strength and weakness of the figure "general will." See a discussion of the question from *The Social Contract* which ends with these words: " . . . no one exists who does not secretly appropriate the term *each* and think of himself when he votes for all?"—in Paul de Man, *Allegories of Reading: Figural Language in Rousseau, Nietzsche, Rilke, and Proust* (New Haven, 1979), 269.

20. "S'interrogea-t-il [Robespierre] sur la loi, effroyablement mystérieuse, qui, depuis l'origine du monde, couronne les artisans le l'iniquité . . ." (2:552).

21. *Origin of Species* (1859) was translated into French in 1862. See Ivette Conry, *L'Introduction de Darwin en France* (Paris, 1975).

NOTES ON THE AUTHORS

PETER BROOKS is Tripp Professor of Humanities and Director
of the Whitney Humanities Center at Yale University. Currently a
National Endowment for the Humanities Fellow, he is the author
of *The Novel of Worldliness*, *The Melodramatic Imagination*,
and *Reading for the Plot*. He is working on a book on narrative
and the body.

PATRICE HIGONNET, Goelet Professor of French History at
Harvard University, is the author of *Class, Ideology, and the
Rights of Nobles during the French Revolution*, and *Sister
Republics: The Origins of French and American Republicanism*.
With Margaret Higonnet he has written on Benjamin Constant
and Mme de Charrière, and is also co-authoring a book on
suicide in eighteenth-century France.

MARIE-HÉLÈNE HUET is William R. Kenan Professor of
Romance Languages at Amherst College. She has published
*Rehearsing the Revolution: The Staging of Marat's Death, 1793-
1797*, as well as several articles on the French Revolution. In 1987
she was the recipient of a grant from the Guggenheim
Foundation for research on Monstrosity and Imagination.

CHRISTIE McDONALD, Professor of French at the University of
Montreal, is the author of *The Extravagant Shepherd: A Study of
the Pastoral Vision in Rousseau's* Nouvelle Héloïse, *The
Dialogue of Writing: Essays in Eighteenth Century Literature*,
and *Dispositions: Quatre essais sur les écrits de Rousseau,
Mallarmé, Proust et Derrida*.

LINDA ORR teaches French literature at Duke University. She
has published *Jules Michelet: Nature, History, and Language*,
and "The Revenge of Literature: A History of History." Her next
book, *Headless History: Nineteenth-Century French Historiography of the Revolution*, is forthcoming.

SANDY PETREY is Professor of French and Comparative
Literature at the State University of New York at Stony Brook.
The author of *Realism and Revolution* and of *History in the
Text: Quatrevingt-Treize and the French Revolution*, he is
currently writing a book on speech acts and literary theory.

JAMES H. RUBIN, Professor of Art at the State University of
New York at Stony Brook, has written *Eighteenth-Century
French Life-Drawing*, *Realism and Social Vision in Courbet and*

Proudhon, and *Eugène Delacroix: 'Dantebarke': Idealismus und Modernität*, as well as numerous articles, including several on the art of revolutionary and post-revolutionary France.

CHANTAL THOMAS, a scholar affiliated with the Centre National de Recherche Scientifique in Lyons, is the author of books on Sade and Casanova. Her most recent publication is *La Reine scélérate: Marie-Antoinette à travers les pamphlets*. She has contributed to several collective works on the French Revolution.